STORMY WINDS

STORMY WINDS

FIRE AND HAIL,
SNOW AND CLOUDS,
STORMY WINDS, FULFILLING
HIS WORD (PSALMS 148:8)

Cassandra Hall

To order additional copies of this book, contact:
Xlibris
UK TFN: 0800 0148620 (Toll Free inside the UK)
UK Local: (02) 0369 56328 (+44 20 3695 6328 from outside the UK)
www.Xlibrispublishing.co.uk
Orders@Xlibrispublishing.co.uk
850010

CONTENTS

DEDICATION

It is with much love and heartfelt appreciation that I dedicate this book to my family at Upper Room Intercessory and Teaching Ministry and At the Feet of Jesus Ministry. Thank you all for your support, steadfastness, and commitment. Thank you all for affording me the honour and privilege to serve you and minister to you over the years.

For those going through the storms and turbulences of life and for those in their midnight hour, hold fast, knowing help is on the way. As you read this book, may you find the strength, courage, and grace to hold on until the storm passes by, knowing that you are safe and secure in God's hands. No matter what you are facing this very moment, rest assured that the promises of God concerning your life and destiny will be fulfilled to the glory of God!

ACKNOWLEDGEMENT

If it had not been the Lord who was and is on my side, where would I have been? I give all glory, honour, and praise to God the Father, God the Son, and God the Holy Spirit! I have come to realise that everything absent of God amounts to nothing; however, God plus nothing equals everything. Lord, I owe You my all, I give You my all. Thank You for Your grace and mercy, Your loving kindness, and Your unconditional love. I thank You, Lord, for being the wind beneath my sail and for guiding me through the storms of life, ensuring that I get to my destination safely and unharmed. My greatest achievement in life is to be called Your servant, child, and daughter.

To Bishop Victoria Araba Beecham of Christian Action Faith Ministries, Action Chapel Milton Keynes Branch, I am grateful to God and grateful to you for your support and love. It is an honour to have you partake of this work of God. I honour you as unto the Lord.

Deaconess Dolly "Mum" London-Taylor, God gave me you and gave you me, and I am forever grateful to Him and grateful to you for your motherly tender loving care, advice, wisdom, and continued support and encouragement. Aside from the Lord, you're a pillar of strength to me.

My sister and dearest friend Juliet Campbell, only the Lord knows how much you have been there for me, selflessly supporting me through challenging times and in good times. I thank God for sharing His gift—you—with me.

FOREWORD

I count it a great honour to write these words as a foreword to this inspirational book by my sister, Rev. Cassandra Hall.

Beyond stormy winds lies purpose.

Nothing is more important than to learn how to maintain a life of purpose in the midst of painful adversity. As you turn these pages, you will frequently hear the voice of God. For some, this book will bring insight and discovery. For others, however, it will evoke a divine call to a lifetime in the ranks of those whom God desires to take beyond adversities. *Warfare surrounds the birth of miracles.* Every sentence of this book is pregnant with wisdom, and I enjoyed the mind-expanding experience of this exciting book. I admonish you to plunge into this ocean of knowledge and watch your storms turn into blessings by God.

Bishop Victoria Beecham
Action Chapel International (UK)
Milton Keynes

INTRODUCTION

Stormy Winds was birthed by the Holy Spirit out of a challenging and difficult time, not only in my life but also in the nations of the world. Many, including myself, are yet to recover from these challenges. However, God, through His word as written in this book, has reassured us that despite it all, despite the long nights and dark seasons, and despite the personal changes and challenges, we, His people, need not fear—His word and promises will be fulfilled in our lives. We need not worry because the Lord is too faithful to fail us, and He will never fail us as long as we rest in Him and His word. *Stormy Winds* is scripture-based and has been put together using the Bible as the main point of reference.

This book highlights to the reader what stormy winds are, how stormy winds present themselves, reasons stormy winds are experienced, and scripture-based revelations and insight as to how one will or can survive, maintaining their focus, faith, and trust in God and His word, as they encounter and go through life's windstorms and trials.

CHAPTER ONE

Have You Considered My Servant?

Have you ever encountered a situation that makes you feel as though you're caught in a raging windstorm with no hope of escape? If you're caught in the turbulence of life, be encouraged that God is working on your behalf to bring to an end, the challenges you're now facing.

One might ask—what are stormy winds? In the natural, the word 'stormy' describes weather conditions that are thunderous, windy with frequent dark clouds, lightning and heavy, pelting rain. Stormy winds can sometimes be described as ill winds, a blizzard or just about any tumultuous weather condition. Whatever the case might be, a stormy wind is an unpleasant situation that is potentially harmful and at times life-threatening.

Many times, as children of God, we'll encounter life's "stormy winds" and tempestuous conditions, that will pose a threat both physically and spiritually. On occasion, we face violent turbulence, greatly disturbed by trials, challenges and temptations, that can be likened to stormy winds.

The Psalmist however, encourages us in Psalm 148:8 that no matter how dark the days, no matter how frigid or piercing the cold, and no matter how difficult the hardship, God's Word will still be fulfilled in our lives. Jesus puts it this way, *"Heaven and earth will pass away, but My word will by no means pass away (Matthew 24:35 NKJV).* In other words, nothing can abort nor nullify the Word of God.

God reminds us that His word is everlasting when He said,

"For as the rain comes down, and the snow from heaven, And do not return there, But water the earth, And make it bring forth and bud, That it may give seed to the sower And bread to the eater, So shall My word be that goes forth from My mouth; It shall not return to Me void, But it shall accomplish what I please, And it shall prosper in the thing for which I sent it. (Isaiah 55:10-11 NKJV). Irrespective of life's stormy winds and weather conditions, God's Word concerning your life, will prosper; it will accomplish that which it was sent to do, as long as we apply scriptural principles and obey His Word and His promises.

When a storm is brewing against us, we can be sure of one thing—that the devil is doing his best to raise the stakes. The devil doesn't do things half way, but carefully considers every eventuality, to increase our odds of injury that will offer him new inroads into our lives. And while using our storms to his advantage, there will also come a time where we end up on the devil's calendar—his next target.

It's like the devil is sitting at a round table with his investigators and special agents asking, "Who's next?" And his special agents respond by telling him that it's you or me. Then once our portfolio is opened and read at the enemy's table, they devise a strategy for a war intentionally aimed at destroying us. A plan is then set in motion, and they launch an attack. Can you picture this in your mind's eye? Bear in mind this scenario is not biblical; it's just for narrative purposes.

One such man I believe this scenario describes is a servant of God called Job. The Bible introduced Job as a man *"blameless and upright, one who feared God and shunned evil."* He was a very wealthy man who owned thousands of sheep, camels, hundreds of oxen and female donkeys, as well as a very large household, which made him *"the greatest of all the people of the East."*

One fateful day, Job's name was next on the demonic calendar. According to the Scriptures, *Now there was a day when the sons of God came to present themselves before the Lord, and Satan also came among them. And the Lord said to Satan, "From where do you come?" So Satan answered the Lord and said, "From going to and fro on the earth, and from walking back and forth on it." Then the Lord said to Satan; "Have you considered My servant Job, that there is none like him on the earth, a blameless and upright man, one who fears God and shuns evil?" (Job 1:6-7 NKJV).*

Satan answered God, *"Does Job fear God for nothing? Have You not made a hedge around him, around his household, and around all that he has on every side? You have blessed the work of his hands, and his possessions have increased in the land. But now, stretch out Your hand and touch all that he has, and he will surely curse You to Your face!" And the Lord said to Satan, "Behold, all that he has is in your power; only do not lay a hand on his person." So Satan went out from the presence of the Lord (Job 1:9-12).*

After considering Job and reading about his faithfulness to God, Satan sought God's permission to destroy him, on the premise that Job's loyalty occurred because God had placed a hedge of protection around him and all that he had. Satan challenged God, saying that the day the Lord removed His hedge from around Job, he would curse the Lord.

The devil's accusation was brought not against God, but against Job. God was willing to risk everything to prove Satan wrong. God told the devil "Fine. He's all yours. Only do not touch his life." Satan was, by then, engaged in a war with God, with Job being used as the battle axe, God would defeat the devil. And even though Job was an instrument of war in the hands of God, he suffered greatly. Just as he did in the case of Job, the enemy still goes around, *"like a roaring lion seeking who he may devour" (1 Peter 5:8)*. At some point in his roaming, he'll set his sights on you and me, for the sole purpose of destroying us, and stripping us of all we possess, both physically and spiritually. Day and night, the devil relentlessly seeks to confuse us, to lead us astray—the beloved of the Lord.

Peter spoke the following, *Beloved, do not think it strange concerning the fiery trial which is to try you, as though some strange thing happened to you; (1 Peter 4:12 NKJV)*. In other words, your storm is nothing strange, and most importantly, it doesn't take God by surprise. God is fully aware of the attacks on your life, finances, ministry, marriage, children and your destiny. For all you know, He has granted the devil permission to strip you of all you have, ultimately, to capture the devil in his own trap.

Jesus Christ was stripped of all he had by the devil. God the Father allowed this, because He was confident in the faithfulness of his Son. In proving His faithfulness to God the Father, Jesus endured all the sufferings, ridicule, pain and shame, for the salvation and deliverance of the human race—you and me. At the end of it all, it was said, *"For had they known, they would not have crucified the Lord of glory" (1 Corinthians 2:8b NKJV)*.

If the devil had known of His dominion and authority, and how Jesus's death would've benefitted mankind, he wouldn't have sought His crucifixion. To apply this in the moment, perhaps you're feeling that you've been stripped of all you have, and everything around you is being destroyed. The next question should be: how faithfully have we endured all that for the greater glory set before you? Can you and I remain faithful even when the devil is allowed to destroy what we have, and bring us to nothing?

Indeed, Job was a wealthy man, blessed on every level. He was a father and a husband, as well as a faithful breadwinner, provider and protector of his family. Undoubtedly, he was a good master to his servants, and a faithful friend to his companions. He was a counsellor to many and a comforter to the broken hearted—one who supported widows and had a seat in a place of honour and influence *(Job 29)*. Job evidently displayed the character and nature of God in all he did.

Then came Satan who took away all that he had and made him a laughing-stock and the object of gossip. It all began with an attack on his character in the form of an accusation, followed by events that I'm sure Job never once thought would happen. It all began on a seemingly normal day when, without warning, a messenger ran up and informed Job that rustlers had raided the field where his oxen fed, and all his servants were killed except the messenger. Before the servant messenger could finish speaking, Job was told by another, *"The fire of God fell from heaven and burnt up the sheep and the servants, and consumed them; and I alone have escaped to tell you!"* *(Job 1:16)*. Whilst this servant was still speaking, he was informed of another raid where his camels were stolen and his servants killed, with the exception of the servant who relayed the message. To add insult to injury, another servant arrived to report that a great wind struck the building, which collapsed and killed all his sons and daughters. Once again, the messenger alone escaped to inform Job of that last, worst catastrophe.

Imagine how broken and devastated Job was by that time. Can you imagine his state of grief and anguish? There was always someone who escaped, to give Job the bad news. In the same way, it seems that there's always someone to remind us of the loss and disastrous events we've faced. We often feel as though we're hearing messages that are more discouraging than encouraging. Discouragement seems to somehow superimpose and overcome every encouraging word, and bury every iota of encouragement. Bad news kept coming at Job without respite, without time for him to absorb the previous bad news and no time to think. Can you imagine this happening to you? Or, is it happening to you right now?

As a righteous man, Job never shouted, "God, why me?" One thing was sure, he never cursed God, though his wife encouraged him to curse God and die. Rather, the Bible tells us,

Then Job arose, tore his robe, and shaved his head; and he fell to the ground and worshiped. And he said: "Naked I came from my mother's womb, and naked I shall return there. The Lord gave, and the Lord has taken away; Blessed be the name of the Lord." In all this job did not sin nor charge God with wrong (Job 1:20-22).

Job shaved his head. He mourned. He fell on his face before God, and acknowledged that the Lord was responsible for giving him every blessing, so it was acceptable if God wanted to take them away if He saw fit. You and I on the other hand, might have cursed God, turned our backs on Him and said all manner of evil words against God. When in our own way we show our disapproval of what God has allowed in our lives, it's as if we turned against Him. How many times have we suffered loss? At some point in our lives we all have lost love, lost relationships, businesses, finances, and the list goes on. Many have cursed both God and man, and we often blame Him for what has been lost. Some go as far as to give up on God by saying there is no God, and wondering why, if there is a God, He allowed such things to happen.

As small children, we may have been hurt by things that happened to us. We might have fallen and hurt ourselves, while others were even involved in accidents that took their lives. Many suffer heartache, neglect, rejection, and abuse of all kinds. And if that's so, is it fair to say that their parents were responsible for all the bad things that happened to them? In the same way, while they might have done a better job of parenting, we don't accuse our parents of not being real because those things happened. In the same way, we dare not blame our heavenly Father for the hurtful things that happened, refusing to believe He's real because He didn't prevent them.

Is it fair to say our parents didn't care about us and were responsible for all the bad things that happened to us? Did you ever say mom and dad weren't real because you suffered many things as a child? No! So why do we blame our heavenly Father for the challenges we are going through, thinking that God is not real and He does not care about us?

Our earthly parents may have allowed us to go through challenges to mature us. They didn't rescue us every time we got into trouble, because it was vital that we learn to extricate ourselves, deciding not to repeat those same foolish behaviours again. Otherwise, some of us would never have learned wisdom. They called it tough love! So why do we behave like babies when God shows us a bit of tough love? We're entirely too quick to brand the Lord as fake before we backslide. When He allows us to go through challenges that are meant to strengthen us and build our faith in Him and His Word, He says He inclines His ear to hear our prayers and runs to meet us when we run to Him. During those times, He's more real and trustworthy than any human parent could ever be, and His love far exceeds the love of our earthly parents.

Answer this question. Did you come into this world with any of the things you now possess? All that you now possess—were those things not given to you by the Lord? The truth is that as children of God, we've achieved nothing in our own strength. Everything we have and all we've accomplished, are gifts of God, who goes beyond giving what is good. He also goes as far as to take away those things which are bad and unproductive for us.

No matter where we find ourselves, God allowed these things for His purposes. He didn't cause them, but He did allow them. In reality, God has the power to stop bad things from happening to us all, however, if they manifest, it's for a purpose. Many times, we're responsible for the situations we're in, but instead of acknowledging it, we shift the blame to God and others. If we fail to admit the truth, that we're the cause of certain stormy winds we face, we'll never get the help we need. Getting out of some storm will mean allowing the Spirit of God to work on us and our character or on certain character traits and addictions that got us in trouble in the first place.

There are times when we find ourselves facing challenges, and God allows them to continue because we refuse to give Him control of that situation. We all have choices to make, and the Lord will by no means forcefully override our choices. That said, there's no way God is to blame for the bad things we experience. Before blaming the Lord, ask yourself if you consulted God or invited Him into the matter. Sometimes, we never touched bases with God, but when things begin to go bad, all of a sudden, we remember He is there and we start the blame game, when He actually had nothing to do with it. Let's not fool ourselves, because God is not mocked.

Once we've surrendered our all to God and are faithful and obedient to Him, He promises to meet us where we are when we call on His name. During those times when He seems far away, He encourages us to continue to trust and obey, without faltering or doubt. Never curse God or blame Him for the misfortunes you suffer, especially when you're in rebellion and walking away from God. God boasted about His faithful servant Job. Can God boast over you and me, knowing that no matter what storms we face, we will continue to trust Him for a good outcome?

Can God trust you and me to remain faithful to Him when things don't go as we plan? Do we still trust God when we're hurting or when He removes things and people from our lives that He knows will destroy us? Sometimes God will remove people from our lives or remove us from a place of comfort, because He knows that if we stay connected to such people or places, it will lead to our downfall. God can see far beyond what we see. Sadly, some still chase after the very things and people God has removed from their lives for their good. Has trusting God become so difficult that we cannot let go of the things and people He has removed from our lives?

Job went through incredible suffering. His wife told him to curse God and die. His flesh was afflicted with diseases. He became pretty much homeless and penniless, and his friends accused him of sinning against God, which they believed had caused all his losses. The people whom he once helped and cared for, saw him looking like a beggar and a vagrant on the street, and they crossed over to the other side, treating him with disgust and contempt. Through it all Job never cursed God. While God allowed Satan to afflict Job's health, he held fast to his integrity in the Lord.

Perhaps you're going through a storm of ill health—and like Job, you're holding fast to your integrity in God. Maybe your marriage just ended after many years of togetherness. Perhaps you just lost a loved one, or your business has gone bankrupt. You might even know believers who are going through some of the same trials, but can you still trust God not to only come through for them, but for yourself as well?

When your friends abandon you and become wicked counsellors to you in your time of need, condemning you because of your circumstances, will you still hold fast to your integrity in God? Will you trust the Lord even when you don't feel Him near you? I pray that you will.

The song writer wrote;

Through it all, through it all
I've learnt to trust in Jesus;
And I've learnt to trust in God
Through it all, through it all
I've learnt to depend upon His Word.
Andrae Crouch

There is a word and a promise that God has given to all of us, and He expects us to depend upon that Word and anchor our faith to His promises—through it all!

Job went through rejection and loneliness, betrayal and loss; so that he cursed the day he was brought forth from his mother's womb (Job 3). He was in bitterness of spirit and soul, yet he did not utter a hateful word against his Maker. You and I are always in the battle plan of God against the devil. Know that what you're going through is a battle for your soul and life's destiny, as well as a battle for the destiny of others. There is a battle going on over your faithfulness and righteousness to God. We dare not surrender and lose this battle, knowing that the Lord is fighting on our behalf.

We are never alone; God is on our side and He's already won not only the battle, but the entire war! Our God cannot be defeated!

Satan has weighed us out for evil, while God has weighed us through the blood of Jesus, for good. A thief doesn't enter the house of a poor man; what would be the point? It's absolutely pointless, because the thief would go out just as he went in—empty-handed. You and I carry the richness of God's kingdom, glory, life, Spirit and the Word within us—that's exactly why the enemy has set his eyes upon us to steal, kill and destroy God's good plan. However, even in the midst of it all, when the devil has gone on the attack, God will preserve His treasure in us, as long as we remain faithful and obedient to Him and His Word.

LATTER BLESSINGS IN YOUR STORM

Before God permitted Satan to touch or destroy all Job had; Let us recall Job 1:1-3

There was a man in the land of Uz, whose name was Job; *and that man was blameless and upright, and one who feared God and* [a] *shunned evil. And seven sons and three daughters were born to him. Also, his possessions were seven thousand sheep, three thousand camels, five hundred yoke of oxen, five hundred female donkeys, and a very large household, so that this man was the greatest of all the* [b]*people of the East.*

Job had

Seven Thousand Sheep
Three Thousand Camels
Five Hundred Yoke of Oxen
Five Hundred Female Donkeys
A very Large Household
Seven Sons and Three Daughters

Remember, Job lost all those blessings at the hand of the enemy. He lost those blessings whilst he was a part of God's battle plan and His instrument of war. Even after the devil was defeated, Job never cursed God and asked to die, despite the fact that he lost everything he owned and loved; in fact, the Bible tells us in *Job 42:12-17 NKJV,*

Now the LORD *blessed the latter days of Job more than his beginning; for he had fourteen thousand sheep, six thousand camels, one thousand yoke of oxen, and one thousand female donkeys. He also had seven sons and three daughters. And he called the name of the first Jemimah, the name of the second Keziah, and the name of the third Keren-Happuch. In all the land were found no women so beautiful as the daughters of Job; and their father gave them an inheritance among their brothers.*

After this Job lived one hundred and forty years, and saw his children and grandchildren for four generations. So Job died, old and full of days.

The Lord blessed the latter days of Job more than his beginning. Job had fourteen thousand sheep
six thousand camels
1000 yoke of oxen
His household doubled; His children and grandchildren were for four generations
Seven sons and three daughters

The Bible goes on to say,

Be glad then, you children of Zion,
And rejoice in the LORD *your God;*
For He has given you the former rain faithfully,
And He will cause the rain to come down for you—
The former rain,
And the latter rain in the first month.

The threshing floors shall be full of wheat,
And the vats shall overflow with new wine and oil.

"So I will restore to you the years that the swarming locust has eaten,
The crawling locust,
The consuming locust,
And the chewing locust,
My great army which I sent among you.
You shall eat in plenty and be satisfied,
And praise the name of the LORD your God,
Who has dealt wondrously with you;
And My people shall never be put to shame. (Joel 2:22-27)

Job experienced famine and desolation, losing everything he loved, but God restored him by giving him back double for his trouble. In the process, God gave Job sheep in a double portion, as well as a double portion of camels and oxen, and a double portion of children and grandchildren for another four generations.

When God decides to bless you after the storm, He not only gives you back all you lost, but He also gives you double what you lost. As you suffer loss throughout the storm, be confident in this: that God is about to bless you with not just what you lost. In fact, He is getting ready to bless you with twice the amount of what you lost.

The prophet Isaiah wrote, *Instead of your shame you shall have* double *honour, And instead of confusion they shall rejoice in their portion. Therefore in their land they shall possess double; Everlasting joy shall be theirs (Isaiah 61:7 NKJV).* This is the promise of God to us: that God would give us double honour and blessings after our shame and reproach. The blessing coming to you is far greater than that which you lost.

In Job 1, his daughters were only termed as Job's three daughters. In *Job 42:13-15* they were named. *And he called the name of the first Jemimah, the name of the second Keziah, and the name of the third Keren-Happuch. In all the land were found no women so* beautiful as the daughters of Job; and their father gave them an inheritance among their brothers. What you thought you lost were the "most beautiful" and the best. However, when God restores all you have lost, you will realise it will be better and greater than you had. Nothing that you once had can be compared with the latter "rain" or latter blessings of God. The new blessings will be more beautiful and bring you greater joy than those you had before. God's appointed weeks of harvest for you at the end of this trial will be far greater than the glory and blessing you lost.

It is said the meaning of JEMIMAH is day by day. Day by day and day after day you will encounter the blessings of God. Hence, the Psalmist David wrote, *"Blessed be the Lord, who daily loads us with benefits, the God of our salvation! Selah (Psalms 68:19 NKJV).* Your salvation shall be day by day, peace—day by day, and joy—day by day; daily you'll experience the manifold blessings of the God who saves and restores you. God will bring you into your JEMIMAH season.

KEZIAH is likened to the word cassia. The cassia is one of the ingredients or spices used in making of the anointing oil in *Exodus 30:22-25*. When God's blessings are restored to you, His fragrance and aroma will fill your life. The fragrance of God will sweeten every area of your life that was once decaying or dead. Isaac said, *"Surely, the smell of my son is like of a field which the Lord has blessed" (Genesis 27:27b NKJV).* Men will smell the blessings of God on the "fields" of your life. God will release fresh anointing and fresh grace upon you!

KEREN-HAPPAUH means "horn of antimony." Antimony is said to be a substance formerly used as an eye cosmetic as in eye shadow. Antimony therefore, was used to enhance beauty. God is about to beautify your countenance that has been downcast, and He's about to change your reflection to one of beauty. In the words of King Solomon, *He has made everything beautiful in its time (Ecclesiastes 3:11a NKJV).* God will make everything beautiful in your life in its time. You shall be and will be, a container of God's beauty; His very own "cosmetic box" that will in turn add beauty to the lives of others.

Isaiah reminds us,

You shall no longer be termed Forsaken,
Nor shall your land any more be termed Desolate;
But you shall be called Hephzibah, and your land Beulah;
For the LORD delights in you,
And your land shall be married (Isaiah 62:4 NKJV).

Like Job's first three daughters who were simply termed his daughters; many times as we go through the storms and trials of life, we are "termed" by our situations, circumstances or even people. We are called forsaken, broken, hurt, wounded, single, lonely or abused. I remind you that this term is used to describe that which is for a time and season, and not something that is permanent. "Term" describes a fixed or limited period for which something is intended to last.

What you are termed as a result of your challenge, also has an expiration date. God is about to name you like the latter three daughters of Job. You're about to be called by the name that carries the original intent and purpose of God for your life. The name by which God will call you is permanent and cannot be tampered with or altered by human beings, situations and circumstances. Focus on what God has called you and not on that which your storm and challenges have "termed" you. There is a name by which you've been called by the Lord in spite of your trials and challenges. For one, you are called blessed and highly favoured by the Lord.

It will be evident for all to see that irrespective of the trials, irrespective of your shortcomings, God still delights in you and is, as it were, still married to you. The common union that you share with the Lord will be proof for all to see. In our storms and challenges people might think like the friends of Job—that the Lord has forsaken us because of some wrong we have committed. But then God will surprise your critics by the fulfilment of His promises to you. David said, *"When my father and mother forsake me, then the Lord will take care of me" (Psalms 27:10 NKJV). Hebrews 13:5b NKJV reads, For He Himself has said, "I will never leave you nor forsake you."* God has never forsaken us and He never will; He is right there waiting for you to invite Him into the storm and grant Him absolute control and authority over, not just some things, but over everything.

Jeremiah 5:24 (NKJV) reads, They do not say in their heart, "Let us now fear the Lord our God, Who gives rain, both the former and the latter, in its season. He reserves for us the appointed weeks of the harvest." Weeks of harvest and God's goodness have been appointed to you by the Lord. A double portion of God's anointing and blessings are coming to you. In fact, God will cause you to forget the hurt, forget the bad news and forget all that the devil has destroyed in your life, setting you up for a greater blessing and a greater reward; if only you can believe.

Job said,

"For there is hope for a tree,
If it is cut down, that it will sprout again,
And that its tender shoots will not cease.
Though its root may grow old in the earth,

And its stump may die in the ground,
Yet at the scent of water it will bud
And bring forth branches like a plant (Job 14:7-9 NKJV). You might be feeling like the plant that's wilting and decaying, yet at the scent of water, and at the release of God's appointed Word which is spirit and life, your life will not only "bud", but bring forth many "branches." Many blessings will flow into your life and from your life, as God's healing streams of life flow into every dead and dying area. God will be faithful as you remain faithful, steadfast, unmovable and unshakeable, in times of the storm.

Before Job's restoration God required one thing of him. He required Job to pray for his friends who sided with Satan to condemn and falsely accuse him. In Job 42:1-10 NKJV we read: *and the* Lord *restored Job's losses when he prayed for his friends. Indeed, the* Lord *gave Job twice as much as he had before.* You too might be where you are because of what others have done to you. The key to Job's blessings was to pray for his friends—those who hurt him. I encourage us all to do the same thing. Matthew 5:44 NKJV admonishes us, *"But I say to you, love your enemies, bless those who curse you, do good to those who hate you, and pray for those who spitefully use you and persecute you."*

CHAPTER TWO

From Potiphar's House to the Palace

It goes without saying that all servants of God have or will pass through some form of challenge or testing before getting to their assigned place in God both spiritually and physically. We can by no means bargain our way out of trials, sufferings and temptations. It's folly for us to think that the life of a believer is exempt from or immune to, suffering. Christ never promised us a rose garden.

He says this: "Even in areas where you made choices that negatively affected your health, I'm releasing forgiveness and restoring what was lost. I'm giving you grace to change your destructive habits and activities this day, for I would that you live long in My Kingdom on the earth, says the Father. I have much for you to do, and I will not allow your years to be shortened. Hear My voice—do what I tell you, and I will restore the strength of your youth. You will run with the footmen and outstrip the horsemen, knowing the vitality and strength of My resurrection life."

He never promised that we would live without struggles. On the contrary, *Jesus said to His disciples, "If anyone desires to come after Me, let him deny himself, and take up his cross, and follow Me" (Matthew*

16:24 NKJV). As we know, the cross is symbolic of suffering. Paul also said, *"For I consider that the sufferings of this present time are not worthy to be compared with the glory which shall be revealed in us" (Romans 8:18 NKJV).* Many Bible passages point to us suffering with Christ. Not only do we suffer with Him, but we're also partakers of the glory that will be revealed.

Let's reacquaint ourselves with the story of the patriarch Joseph who, like Job, went through his fair share of suffering, trials and temptation for the sole purpose of fulfilling his divine mandate. We also read of the boy Joseph who had a dream of greatness as revealed to him by the Lord. Without realizing it was a bad idea, he mentioned the dream to his brothers who were jealous and hated him even more, because he was his father's favourite son. In fact, his father had made him a coat of many colours that was different from the ones they wore. Can you imagine their jealousy, envy and hatred when they saw once again that he was their father's favourite? Time and again they unashamedly displayed their hatred for Joseph. On the other hand, upon hearing his dream, his father *"kept the matter in his mind."*

One fateful day Joseph's brothers were tending to their father's flock, when Jacob sent Joseph to ascertain if all was well with them. Upon seeing Joseph some distance away, *they conspired against him to kill him,* and planned to inform his father that he was killed by a wild animal.

His brother, Rueben, urged them not to kill him, but to cast him into a pit. However, before casting him into the pit, the rest of his brothers stripped him of the multicoloured tunic. When they sat down to eat, the brothers saw a company of Ishmaelites on route to Egypt bearing many spices. His brother, Judah, then suggested that he be sold to the Ishmaelites, and in the end, they sold Joseph for thirty shekels of silver.

Reuben, who ultimately wanted to return Joseph to his father, later arrived at the pit and when he found that Joseph was gone, he tore his clothes in anguish. He returned to his brothers and told them that Joseph was no more; they hadn't revealed to Reuben that they had sold Joseph to the Ishmaelites, but instead, let him believe he was already dead. Together, *they took Joseph's tunic, killed a kid of the goats and dipped the tunic in the blood (Genesis 37:31, NKJV).* His bloody tunic was then presented to his father, along with the lie about his death. Joseph's brothers watched their father break down and desperately mourn for his beloved son. They even tried to comfort their father, but never once admitted their lies. How wicked was that?

The ones to whom Joseph was sold then sold him to a man named Potiphar, who *was an officer of Pharaoh and captain of the guard (See Genesis 37).* Now a slave, Joseph went from one trial to another, with no end in sight. However, I believe that, like Job, he held onto his integrity and trusted in God for his future.

Is this not a rather interesting beginning for one to whom God had revealed greatness? Take a moment to recall what great things God has promised you from His Word and through the words of His servants, and that which He has spoken to you directly by His Spirit. Also, compare what God has revealed to you, about the place where you are, at the moment. Let this be a moment of contemplation of God's great goodness to you.

God told Joseph he would make him great in the sight of his brothers and parents. This prophetic word carried a seal of his greatness in the form of the tunic of many colours his father made for him. Even if Joseph hadn't revealed his dream to his brothers, I believe the tunic spoke volumes to his siblings who needed no other excuse to be rid of him. The coat alone was evidence that his father loved and favoured him above them all, and that he carried a blessing that set him apart for greatness and honour. His tunic was most likely similar to those worn by royals. The tunic was his father's token of love which the Lord also had for his servant Joseph. This prophetic seal alongside his revealed dream, marked the genesis of troubles and storms for a young man destined for greatness.

The great blessing of God upon your life will always attract adversities. Whether you mention it or not, the devil knows it. There is always a seal of God's greatness and approval upon our lives that others will see without a word from us. When we speak about the things God has revealed to us concerning our destinies, and that which He is doing in our lives, it will always attract envy and jealousy, emphasizing to others their own inadequacies. Let's be real. Not everyone will be happy with where God is taking us.

Paul instructs us, *"Rejoice with those who rejoice, and weep with those who weep" (Romans 12:15 NKJV)*. Interestingly enough, though we are commanded to rejoice in the Lord, we often struggle to do that, distracted by the struggles we face. However, God desires us not only to rejoice always, but to rejoice with those who rejoice. Likewise, we should mourn or weep with those who weep. We should partake of both the joy and sorrows of one another.

Interestingly enough, the adversity will sometimes start in our very household; it will begin with our family members, friends and loved ones, work colleagues and even those in the church. David said,

For it is not an enemy *who* reproaches me;
Then I could bear it.
Nor is it one *who* hates me who has exalted *himself* against me;
Then I could hide from him.
But it was you, a man my equal,
My companion and my acquaintance.

We took sweet counsel together,

And walked to the house of God in the throng *(Psalms 55: 12-14 NKJV).* Jesus Himself once said, *"And a man's enemies will be that of his own household" (Matthew 10:36 NKJV).* Therefore, this should come as no surprise to us—that the source of stormy winds can be those we love, cherish, look up to, trust and respect the most.

How many times have we encountered and experienced betrayal from those we love? How many times have we shared visions with those we think are for us and we are undermined, hated and despised as a result? How many become our enemies when God wants to promote us? How many times has God opened great and effective doors to us, as he did for Paul, yet we find many adversaries behind those doors? *(1 Corinthians 16:9).* These adversaries are sometimes surprisingly and sadly, the ones closest to us.

There are those who, out of so-called love for us, would rather have us continue with them in the things that displease God, rather than cheering on and assisting us on our journey with God. All these are enemies of our progress in God and bad weeds in our lives, that are knowingly or unknowingly positioned, to lead us along a rocky or stormy path.

What do we do when adversities arise? Do adversities have a positive purpose? While Joseph was in the pit, I believe he was praying a prayer much like Job a man who was all too familiar with stormy winds, who wrote*: When they cast you down, and you say, 'Exaltation will come!" Then He will save the humble person. (Job 22:29 NKJV)*

While Joseph was praying in the pit, I doubt that he imagined he would once again be sold into bondage. I suspect he thought he'd be delivered, free again to return to his father and the life he knew and loved. Joseph was saved from the pit, but was sold into Potiphar's household. Whilst serving Potiphar and his household, Potiphar saw that the Lord was with Joseph. He then looked favourably upon him and made Joseph overseer over his house and all his affairs. During that time the Lord also blessed the house of Potiphar for Joseph's sake. From the pit to Potiphar's house might have at first seemed to be a place of bondage for this servant of God; however, in the end, it became his place of exaltation.

Many times, God might deliver us from one challenge, and like Joseph, we immediately end up facing another. Yet whilst facing that trial, God can still bless and favour us just as He did Joseph. If you keep your focus on the Lord in the midst of your storm, God will unveil His blessings to you, even in a seemingly bad situation. Sometimes His blessings are right in front of us, though we just can't see them because our focus is on the storm instead of the Lord.

All was going well for Joseph, which can also happen to us. Out of a bad situation we can encounter the goodness of God. Whilst serving his master, the Bible tells us,

Now Joseph was handsome in form and appearance. And it came to pass after these things that his master's wife cast longing eyes on Joseph, and she said, "Lie with me" (Genesis 39:6b-7 NKJV).

Joseph repeatedly rejected her attempts at seduction. One day Potiphar's wife tried to seduce Joseph and he fled from her grip, leaving his cloak in her hand.

Sadly, for Joseph, because he had no other witness to the event, he was found guilty of a crime he didn't commit and was thrown into prison, no doubt shocked at this undeserved turn of events. Just after his exaltation had finally come, he once again faced heartache in prison with no end in sight.

The Bible reveals something very interesting in this passage. Whilst Joseph was prospering in a situation that was meant to suppress him, he caught the attention of Potiphar's wife. *His master's wife cast longing eyes on Joseph.* It's clear that when we're prospering, even after being "sold" into situations that are meant to destroy us, we will attract the devil's attention. At that point, he turns his attention to ways he can turn things around for our harm.

The aim of the enemy is for us to remain at the bottom of the barrel, down-trodden and destitute. However, even then, God's plan is for us is to be above and not beneath—for us to be victors rather than victims of our circumstances. As in the case of Joseph, when the devil is seeking to destroy us, he will make sure we're alone, with no witnesses—no one to vouch for our character.

However, Jeremiah 42:5 says, *So they said to Jeremiah, "Let the LORD be a true and faithful witness between us, if we do not do according to everything which the LORD your God sends us by you."* As you weather your stormy winds, many might have accused you, sown all manner of falsehood against you and said things to discredit you in the eyes of others. As a result, you might find yourself isolated. Even when the facts point to your guilt, we know facts can be skewed so things appear true, when they're in error.

Human beings might be absent in the midst of your storm, but God's Holy Spirit is your true and faithful witness, who will vindicate you in His time. Revelation 1:5a says this: *"And from Jesus Christ, the faithful witness, the first born from the dead."* No matter what storms you're now facing, Jesus Christ is your faithful witness, who will vouch for you and deliver you in the end. Jesus Christ, the Word of God and His promises, are always with us to bear record of our innocence, when like Joseph, we're facing unlawful charges. And while you might ask why God allowed it to happen, just know that God has a greater plan that far exceeds what we can dream or imagine if we simply hold onto faith and believe He is in the process.

According to *Genesis 39:1-6;* the Lord had blessed Joseph in Potiphar's house. However, He wanted to move Joseph from a glorified servant in Potiphar's house and set him to rule over a nation. He wanted him to get to Pharaoh.

To get to Pharaoh, Joseph had to go through the captain of Pharaoh, hence, the Lord allowed him to go through Potiphar's house. But God never wanted Joseph to be comfortable there when He had indeed called Joseph to greatness in Egypt. So, God allowed circumstances to move him out of that comfort zone into the place of his destiny.

The officer—Potiphar, was in a place of prominence under Pharaoh, so it was to Joseph's advantage for him to dine with Pharaoh. When God takes us to greater heights in Him, during times of divine shifting, He will make us uncomfortable where we are until we're okay with moving on. At times, we may find that our lives are disrupted by betrayal, lies, rejection, etc. And suddenly we, like Joseph, find ourselves being plunged into another unexpected trial. After a brief moment of being "lifted up", we find ourselves going down for the third time, unsure we'll survive it.

The Shunammite woman in *2 Kings 8:1-6,* had lost everything and was in the land of the Philistines during a time of famine. That was the storm that drove her to the land of the Philistines. After the famine ended, she went to the king to appeal that her house and land be restored to her. In fact, this is a woman to whom God sent Elisha to not only bless her with a son, but to eventually raise her son from the dead. *(See 2 Kings 4:8-37.)*

On approaching the king, Elisha's servant, Gehazi, spoke to the king about what God had used the prophet Elisha to do in the woman's life. Upon seeing her, Gehazi said to the king, *"My Lord, O king, this is the woman, and her son who Elisha restored to life."* The Bible went on to say that, upon confirmation from the woman, the king appointed a certain officer, saying, *"Restore all that was hers, and all the proceeds of the field from the day that she left the land until now" (2 Kings 8:5-6).* When God wants to restore all you lost, He will, as it were, appoint a "certain officer" to bring about certain opportunities. Yet He might not want us to get too comfortable with the "certain officer", because once that purpose is fulfilled, the Lord will move us on before we become too dependent on that person.

Sometimes relationships fail, friendships fail, and the blessings you had, simply come to an end. If that's so, take heart, for God has a greater plan for you. These people, relationships or opportunities might only be "officers" temporarily appointed in your life to propel you to "pharaoh's palace" or your destiny. They might only be a part of your restoration process, and not the completion of God's restoration process, so hold them lightly, ready to move when God says to go.

At times your lifting up might involve being cast down again for a season, before getting to your ultimate destiny. For a season, life might appear to be like a role play—same script, different characters, filled with many déjà vu moments. Joseph was cast into prison after the accusation, cast into a low place after his relationship with Potiphar ended.

What did Joseph do during storms? What do we do in such challenging and stormy times? The first thing we must not do is to question the Lord in a negative way. In our humanness we often find this very difficult. There's nothing wrong with asking the

Lord where we've gone wrong, in order for Him to lead us along the right path. However, many times we tend to ask the Lord, "Why me? Why me? Why now? Why all of a sudden is this happening to me? Why did You allow this, Lord?" "Lord, You promised me this! Lord, you promised me that!" And the lamentations go on and on.

Joseph went from being hated and envied by his brothers, cast into a pit, written off as dead and sold into slavery, to being repeatedly accused and imprisoned, yet he maintained an excellent spirit at all times. The Bible tells how King Saul resented David, nonetheless, *David behaved wisely in all his ways, and the Lord was with him (1 Samuel 18:14)*. I believe that, like David, Joseph behaved wisely in all his ways. As a result, the Lord was with Joseph to order and direct his steps from the pit to Potiphar's house, then to move him into his final destination—Pharaoh's palace where he became ruler over a nation.

Not once have we read in God's Word, where Joseph questioned the Lord, tried to defend himself or resented his trials. In response to storms, our basic instinct is to defend ourselves or try to solve the matter our own way. In so doing, we're prone to behaving unwisely and out of character to prove our point, or to get back at those who offended us. Joseph, on the other hand, took his trials with grace, and even went to prison without rebelling.

Knowing God is working on our behalf and in us, we ought to learn to behave wisely in all things. We ought to petition God for wisdom, then to listen and obey what He says to do in every situation, whether good or bad. We need godly wisdom to remain quiet and to allow God to work on our behalf until He says to do otherwise. In the midst of his storm and turmoil, I believe all Joseph did was to meditate on the promises of God and the dream he had from the Lord. Against all odds, he believed in the faithfulness of God to rescue and deliver him one more time. Joseph kept his gaze fixed on the One who is said to be the author and the finisher of our faith *(Hebrews 12:2)*. He is a positive example to follow as we pass through the stormy winds of life.

Joseph was persuaded that no matter what the issue, his help would come from the Lord. This should be our confession no matter where we find ourselves. Be confident in this one thing: God is working to position you for promotion in Christ Jesus. A greater assignment and blessing is on the way, so don't despair. Continue to look to the hill from whence comes your help, confident that help will come from the Lord *(Psalms 121)*.

According to *Genesis 39:21-25 and Genesis 40,* whilst in prison, God still blessed and favoured Joseph, who still operated in the gift of God. He interpreted a dream that led to the restoration of Pharaoh's chief butler who was also in prison. Upon the restoration of the butler; Joseph requested of him, *"But please remember me when it is well with you, and please show kindness to me; make mention of me to Pharaoh, and get me out of this house" (Genesis 40:14 NKJV).* In his humanness, the butler who God allowed to be thrown in prison, forgot Joseph when he was out of prison and restored to his position.

Even in prison, God had appointed another person who was a part of His restoration plan for Joseph. In prison was the man who was ordained to complete God's divine plan for His servant. Joseph was a man of wisdom who knew this as evidenced by the prophetic request he made of the chief butler. Is God not great! In the midst of your trials and temptations God can appoint someone who is at the same place and going through the same challenge you are, to be the one to aid in your deliverance and the establishment of His will for your life!

Don't despise those who are imprisoned with you. For all you know there is one amongst the many, whom God has chosen as your divine helper. Never look down on others because they are afflicted and challenged as you are. God can use any vessel He chooses, to bless us. This is why in praying for our helpers, we need to pray them out of bondage and all forms of imprisonment. For all you know, your divine helper is in bondage somewhere and unable to assist in your release until you release them with prayers of faith.

Never despise your pit or prison, as the pit or prison is also assigned to get you to your final destination. The "officer"—Potiphar could only take Joseph so far, but it was from prison that he was about to connect with his divine destiny. I'm amazed that despite all Joseph went through, God blessed him no matter what his situation. God confirmed to His servant who trusted in Him that he was still blessed and prosperous no matter where he was, because Joseph carried the very presence of God. There he operated in his calling and found favour with both God and man. First, he was an overseer and a leader in Potiphar's house and

then an overseer and a leader even in prison. Joseph's confirmation of greatness and the prophetic word for his life, followed him, even in bondage. Do you not think this is possible in your life also? God is the same yesterday, today and forever and is able to do for us just as He did for Joseph, and even much more for His glory.

Sometimes our imprisonment is for the promotion of another and not just for our benefit. At times those who are appointed to get us out of prison and help us to our final destination, might forget us at their time of breakthrough. However, if that happens, we're not to respond in anger, but treat them kindly as unto the Lord. Life's journey carries many lessons that will aid us in getting to our destiny.

For Joseph, it came to pass after two years; Pharaoh had a dream concerning the nation of Egypt that none of the wise men in all Egypt could interpret. Suddenly, the chief butler remembered Joseph who had once interpreted his dream of being restored to his position before Pharaoh. *Then the chief butler spoke to Pharaoh, saying: "I remember my faults this day"* (Genesis 41:9 *NKJV*). The chief butler told Pharaoh how Joseph had correctly interpreted his dream while in prison, and Pharaoh immediately sent for Joseph, who correctly interpret Pharaoh's dream *that indeed there will be seven years of great plenty will come throughout all the land of Egypt; but after them seven years of famine will arise, and all the plenty will be forgotten in the land of Egypt: and the famine will deplete the land (Genesis 41:29-30).*

He also gave Pharaoh wise counsel which enabled the nation of Egypt to prosper, ultimately preserving lives during the upcoming years of famine. Upon accurate interpretation of Pharaoh's dream by the inspiration of God, Pharaoh appointed Joseph over the land of Egypt! Upon recognizing that God was with Joseph, Pharaoh said, *"Inasmuch as God has shown you all this, there is* no one as discerning and wise as you. You shall be over my house, and all my people shall be ruled according to your word; only in regard to the throne will I be greater than you." *And Pharaoh said to Joseph, "See, I have set you over all the land of Egypt" (Genesis 41:39-41 NKJV).*

After this, Pharaoh placed his signet ring on Joseph's hand, clothed him in fine garments and put a gold chain around his neck *(See Genesis 41).* A nation and a people bowed before Joseph as he rode by in his chariot. What an awesome story of a man who suffered greatly before getting promoted to his rightful place of destiny, as predestined by God. At your appointed time, God will cause those appointed as your helpers to remember you. In less than twenty-four hours, everything changed for Joseph after a seemingly endless trial. God can and is about to do the same for us.

Joseph might have been stripped of his tunic of many colours, but in the end, God clothed him in a royal robe and granted him in the natural, the place that had been prophesied in the spirit realm. His dream finally came true when God's prophetic revelation was made manifest against all odds! Your storm might have stripped you of your identity in God, and maybe even your peace and joy. You may be feeling vulnerable and exposed to the devices of the wicked, but get ready because God is about to re-clothe you with His seal of your prophetic destiny. His Word concerning you has been settled in heaven (the spirit realm), and is soon about to be made manifest in the natural, if only you believe, and begin to take a godly approach to your storms.

Joseph's greatness culminated in a family reunion after his brothers were sent to Egypt by their father Jacob, to buy grain during a famine *(See Genesis Chapters 42 to 46 for further readings)*. Once Joseph revealed his identity, he forgave their abuse:

"But now, do not therefore be grieved or angry with yourselves because you sold me here; for God sent me before you to preserve life. For these two years the famine has been in the land, and *there are* still five years in which *there will be* neither plowing nor harvesting. *And God sent me before you to preserve a posterity for you in the earth, and to save your lives by a great deliverance. So now it was* not you *who* sent me here, but God; and He has made me a father to Pharaoh, and lord of all his house, and a ruler throughout all the land of Egypt" *(Genesis 45:5-8 NKJV)*.

Joseph then went on to say, *"But as for you, you meant evil against me; but* God meant it for good, in order to bring it about as *it is* this day, to save many people alive" *(Genesis 50:20 NKJV)*. What a display of honour, nobility and integrity! No wonder he was able to behave wisely through his on-going trials. He saw nothing as the work of men or the enemy; rather he saw the moving of the Lord.

I wonder how we look at our trials. Can we choose to see our trials as the work of the Lord for the greater good of others?

The servant of God made known to his brothers that God allowed them to do all they had done to him, for the ultimate preservation of their lives and those of a people and a nation. Can you and I truly accept our troubles as God's will, in order that we too might save the lives of others, including those who have hurt and wounded us? During every step of his arduous journey, Joseph saw God's hand moving him to the land of Egypt not only to make him a ruler over the land, but to preserve the lives of those who sent him there.

This man displayed and demonstrated the love, mercy and forgiveness of God! When we get to our "palace" or appointed place of blessing, will we, like Joseph, be able to forgive those God used to propel us to that position? Are you willing to accept and believe that God is turning it around for your good? Or will we still despise those God has used to betray us, moving us into His divine will and purpose for our lives?

If only you and I can see our challenges as the vehicles which God uses to get us to the successful end of our journeys, we would be able to conduct ourselves wisely at all times and not be offended by God or others who play a role in our eminent success. Their roles might be evil and yes, God allowed them to carry out their schemes, but the fact is they play a vital part in getting us where God wants us to be. The stormy winds are actually blowing you in the direction of God's will and purpose for your life! It's all about our mindset, and seeing God working all things for our good.

In conclusion, Joseph was *handsome in form and appearance (Genesis 39:6c)*. He was well built. In spiritual parlance, he was built up in God, His Word and in faith. Joseph was fortified in God! He was handsome; he reflected the beauty, purity, and holiness of the Lord.

Potiphar's wife noticed him. She saw the beauty of God and how strong he was in the Lord; then she sought for a way she might defile him.

Just as it happened in the case of Joseph and Job, the devil will always take notice of who we are, and he will seek to destroy that beauty and to break us down. Potiphar's wife had his garment in her hands. The facts were there, but the truth is that he was innocent. Men will sentence you because of seemingly incontrovertible facts, but God will deliver you because of truth. The truth by which God will vindicate and deliver us is not based upon what we have or haven't done, or what others say we have or haven't done. Rather, our vindication and deliverance will be based upon His written and spoken word of truth concerning that which He has promised us—upon that which He has called, predestined and preordained us to be in His kingdom.

The song writer wrote,

You are my refuge
You are my sanctuary
When I feel afraid
You're my hiding place
You are my refuge
And when the storm is raging
Underneath Your wings
I rejoice and sing
You are my refuge
Matthew Ward

God will always be a refuge to us when storms are raging like great waves. Trust the Lord and trust His process for your life, because God isn't finished with you yet! He's actually working on your behalf even now. Take shelter in His Word and promises. Hide in Him when you feel afraid. Rejoice always, knowing that God will not allow you to become a casualty of diabolical storms and diverse troubles.

Joseph saw the greater good of God in his pain and storm. So, choose to see the greater good of God during your challenging times and seasons. You might be "sold" by others and by circumstances into what appears to be "slavery" and bondage. Nevertheless, like Joseph, remember you're being sent by God. Your stormy winds and pain are taking you to your divine destination.

Chapter Three

We Have an Issue

Like Job, Joseph and so many others, we're all dealing with issues. The fact that we have an issue, separates us from family, friends and even the will of God. Many are dealing with issues that isolate them, leaving them feeling lonely, rejected and ashamed, as if they're under house arrest. And whether they're aware of it or not, it's like living in isolation, that shuts out everyone and everything else!

The Bible mentions one woman who led a life of isolation, loneliness and rejection because of a physical ailment—an issue of blood. In those days, those issues actually forced women to stay away from others. The Gospel of Mark put it this way:

Now when Jesus had crossed over again by boat to the other side, a great multitude gathered to Him; and He was by the sea. And behold, one of the rulers of the synagogue came, Jairus by name. And when he saw Him, he fell at His feet and begged Him earnestly, saying, "My little daughter lies at the point of death. Come and lay Your hands on her, that she may be healed, and she will live." So Jesus went with him, and a great multitude followed Him and thronged Him.

Now a certain woman had a flow of blood for twelve years, and had suffered many things from many physicians. She had spent all that she had and was no better, but rather grew worse. When she heard about Jesus, she came behind Him in the crowd and touched His garment. *For she said, "If only I may touch His clothes, I shall be made well."*

Immediately the fountain of her blood was dried up, and she felt in her body that she was healed of the affliction. And Jesus, immediately knowing in Himself that power had gone out of Him, turned around in the crowd and said, "Who touched My clothes?" (Mark 5:21–39)

Jesus, who had been in a boat, disembarked and stayed on the seashore, where crowds had already gathered, when a synagogue official by the name of Jairus, approached Him and fell at His feet, clearly upset. He went on to say that his daughter was ill and at the point of death, and he needed Jesus to come and lay hands on her.

As Jesus accompanied Jairus, the Bible tells us that the multitude followed Him. As a leader of the synagogue, Jairus is no different than leaders in the church today, who face desperate issues that need the intervention of Jesus. And just as they do today, people tend to follow along, when these kinds of things happen, to see how Jesus will respond.

Perhaps you're facing a desperate situation and you know people are watching. The question then is, during those times, will we confess that Jesus is Lord over the situation, or will we fall apart and begin to doubt His faithfulness? If this describes your circumstances, it's time to crush doubt and stand in faith, decreeing and declaring that His promises never fail, if we simply choose to believe.

As Jairus sought help for his deteriorating situation, Jesus was faced with a woman who had been haemorrhaging for twelve years, suffering through many medical treatments, and spending all she had. At that point, we might wonder: did Jairus grow anxious and irritated when this woman delayed Jesus' from healing his daughter? We'll never know, but it raises the question: How would we respond if Jesus delayed the healing we seek, to address the needs of someone else? We must remember that in the sight of God, someone else may need His attention before He addresses our issues. His timing is perfect and He knows the future. He's never too early or too late. Even in the case of death, He's able to raise the dead, so we must simply trust that He has our best interest at heart, and He's working on our behalf.

God will never disregard the desperate or dying who cry out for His help, but neither does He react with panic or urgency, when we humans do. Though He might tarry, He never looks at our needs as less important than someone else's. He knows how much we can bear, and is mindful of our individual times and seasons. In fact, Peter says, *"Of a truth I perceive that God is no respecter of persons" (Acts 10:34 KJV)*. In other words, there is no favouritism or partiality in God.

The haemorrhaging woman was only one of many who followed Jesus to Jairus' house, but she caught His attention when she reached out and touched the hem of His garment in faith. This confirms the fact that no matter what hindrances present themselves, Jesus is still on His way to your house. He is already with you in your grief, pain or trials, still on route to you.

You might be wondering if your issue is not urgent in the sight of God, or if He sees you as less desperate than someone else. The Bible says that Jairus approached Jesus and earnestly begged Him, *"Come and lay Your hands on her, that she may be healed, and she will live."* On the other hand, by faith, the woman reached out and touched His garment. This demonstrates to us two levels of prayer that when understood, can help us in our approach to the deliverance we seek.

In his approach, Jairus went to Jesus and said, "Come." Jairus summoned the Lord to tend to his need. This demonstrated the prayer of petition, because he had neither barrier nor opposition to go through to get to Christ. Though this type of prayer has its place, for the purpose of teaching, his petition seemed to be based on entitlement. "Jesus, I am the ruler of the synagogue. I have a dying daughter, so come." "I am a pastor or a bishop or a faithful tither or church goer, so come." "In fact, I'm a child of God and have a desperate situation, so please come."

As mentioned earlier, the woman with issue of blood was, by law, isolated from society and deemed as unclean, and disobedience carried a societal and cultural sentence of death by stoning. According to the Levitical law

'If a woman has a discharge, and the discharge from her body is blood, she shall be set apart seven days; and whoever touches her shall be unclean until evening. *Everything that she lies on during her impurity shall be unclean; also everything that she sits on shall be unclean. Whoever touches her bed shall wash his clothes and bathe in water, and be unclean until evening. And whoever touches anything that she sat on shall wash his clothes and bathe in water, and be unclean until evening. If anything* is on *her* bed or on anything on which she sits, when he touches it, he shall be unclean until evening. *And if any man lies with her at all, so that her impurity is on him, he shall be unclean seven days; and every bed on which he lies shall be unclean (Leviticus 15:19–24 NKJV, chapter 15).*

Can you imagine what it was like for this woman who bled not for seven days as per her customary impurity, but twelve years? Can you imagine how isolated and dirty she felt all those years? Unlike

Jairus, she had to go beyond cultural barriers and societal laws, to breech the rules that prevented her from receiving the blessing reserved for others.

Because of her issue, she had to push beyond the limitations of the enemy and the reasoning of men that disqualified her from that for which she longed. Her issue of blood meant that she had to push through barriers that disqualified her from getting to Jesus. Her issue held her captive, saying, "You may have what it takes to be a wife and a mother, but you're disqualified because of your ailment."

The woman had a variety of issues to press through; she faced much opposition before she finally got to Jesus. In fact, she could have died a gruesome and painful death by stoning had anyone in the crowd noticed her. However, she had made up her mind to press forward toward the Deliverer who was now close enough to touch. Unlike the prayer of Jairus, her prayer was one of travail. She had to push beyond both visible and invisible walls caused by her disability.

Like Jairus, we might only need to petition Jesus to come and He comes, simply because there is no barrier to get through. However, there will be times when we need to travail long and hard in order to break through human, societal, governmental and emotional barriers, that could disqualify us from receiving the healing, breakthrough and deliverance we need.

Maybe the storms, issues and dying situations you are facing are not shifting but rather getting worse, all because it will require travailing in prayer to break through. Go beyond "Come, Jesus," and push through the obstacles that are hindering you from being intimate with God and men (as in human beings). Press against that which is keeping you isolated, alone, condemned, scorned and rejected by others. Break down the walls that are blocking you from being what God has called you to be. Break down and destroy the lies and arguments that say you're disqualified from the promises of God. What issue has defiled you? Rise above it and begin to travail until that issue is no more.

Let's not go to God based on entitlement. Even our entitlement is by His grace, because we've been blessed with His great salvation. The woman pressed in, travailing against all odds and finally got to Jesus. Press beyond the issue that challenges your dreams and hinders your every move. Push forcefully in prayer against that which is draining you of the abundant life of God that you have so longed to enjoy. Travail beyond the issue that has forced you to remain alone and isolated at the back of the crowd. Ask God for the strength she had, to break out of mental shackles that are keeping you bound.

Desperate issues are forcing many to hide in the rear—never reaching their full potential in God. Our expression of intimacy with God and others is hindered and prevented by stormy winds. Desperation has exhausted the can-do fighting spirit of the warrior, so that many are forced into hiding, timid, fearful and ashamed.

The woman with the issue of blood haemorrhaged 365 days a year—without relief for a total of 4,380 days. Every day she faced endless cramps, pain and embarrassment. Every day she got up feeling defiled and fearful of being soiled by her flow. She suffered personal and emotional pain, inconvenience and daily discomfort, and was no doubt growing weary in her efforts to find solutions not only to the issue itself, but to its ramifications.

Rather than being encouraged and supported by her community, she was labelled unclean, and to add insult to injury, the religious community—the church, rejected and isolated her. What emotional torture, pain and anguish she must have suffered. She was in bitterness of soul and no doubt wept many tears. If tears were raindrops, they would, no doubt, have flooded the entire community. How heavy was the burden she'd carried for twelve years, yet she had no one to help carry the load. In the end, she was socially, physically and spiritually bankrupt. To make matters worse, her condition was deteriorating, getting worse by the day. To put it bluntly, she was heading beyond "rock bottom."

What "issue" are you experiencing that causes you pain, grave discomfort, personal and emotional inconvenience, facing rejection, and feeling dirty and isolated? You might be looking for relief and growing weak, exhausted and weary because you've yet to find the answer you seek. Friends, family, loved ones and others might even scorn you and label you a product of your situation. You might be craving intimacy and affection but feel too defiled to reach out to anyone, because of the possibility of rejection.

Sometimes we look to the church for solutions, instead discovering that even in church, we're treated like an outcast. What do you do when you're being drained of the life of God and you are haemorrhaging in various areas of your life? Like the woman with the issue of blood, you who have an issue, seize this moment to reach out to Jesus Christ. Move out of isolation and hiding. Cross the threshold of seclusion and reach out and touch the Lord and Saviour you have come to know. Speak to the Lord this very minute. Be open and honest with the Lord. No man can help with the issues you are experiencing; only God can! He can speak to you and send help through someone else. However, He's the only source of help and your first point of contact for help.

You might have isolated yourself from the house of God—the church, because of your issues. I encourage you to go back. This time seek only Jesus, believing and trusting only Him. Make your salvation a one-on-one experience. Don't focus on how others have treated you; no one is perfect. Remember, others too have issues that Jesus is mindful of and tending to. Focus on touching Jesus and having an intimate relationship with Him.

The woman said, *"If only I may touch His clothes, I shall be made well."* She didn't desire to touch the flesh of Jesus; instead she focused on touching His garment. What a level of faith we see in this woman, who remains unidentified in Scripture. In ancient times the corner of a person's garment represented his identity, and was a symbol of who he was and what he stood for. Naomi, the mother-in-law of Ruth, said to her, *"Then it shall be, when he lies down, that you shall notice the place where he lies; and you shall go in, uncover his feet, and lie down; and he will tell you what you should do" (Ruth 3:4 NKJV).*

When seeking marriage, Ruth uncovered the feet of Boaz and lay there, by the corner or hem of his garment. This was a symbolic request, asking Boaz to identify himself with her. She desired to take on his identity in marriage. In touching the garment of Christ, the woman touched who Jesus was and is, and ultimately, what He stood for. Jesus wears a garment that bears His manifold identities as Lord, Saviour, Peace, Deliverer, Redeemer, Righteousness, Healer, Provider, our Banner, Sanctifier and so much more. Whatever we need, Jesus' garment identifies Him as that to us.

The woman needed to be healed, so she reached out and touched who Jesus was and is—Jehovah Rapha, the God who heals. The garment is Christ, and Christ is the garment; they are inseparable. Jesus is one with the garment filled with the power of His identity. Jesus and His Word are one; all you need to do is to press into the Word and promise of Christ by faith and receive your deliverance.

This woman who had no identity or name in scripture, and was termed "the woman with the issue of blood", received an identity after she touched Christ. The scriptures read, *But His disciples said to Him, "You see the multitude thronging You, and You say, 'Who touched*

Me?"" And He looked around to see her who had done this thing. But the woman, fearing and trembling, knowing what had happened to her, came and fell down before Him and told Him the whole truth. And He said to her, "Daughter, your faith has made you well. Go in peace, and be healed of your affliction."

Not only was she immediately healed after touching and agreeing with whom Jesus said He was to us—our Healer; she was also made whole. And what's more, Jesus said, *"Go in peace."* She went seeking to be healed. However, with her healing came the peace of God. This is important to know because one can be healed or delivered out of an issue or situation, while peace is not necessarily guaranteed, especially if our deliverances are of men and not of God.

When we're healed and delivered by the Lord, our peace is guaranteed. Her issue of blood dried up immediately after touching the garment of Christ when He nullified her old identity, exchanging it for a new one. From that point on, she could do things she'd only dreamt of and access public places without fear of rejection, abuse or death. In fact, she could now embrace the intimacy she so desperately longed for—all because she touched, encountered and embraced Jesus—the very Word of God Himself!

Your change will come not only when you press in and believe, but when you accept and embrace His Word by faith. There is a promise in the Word of God that holds the identity you now seek. If you can only touch the hem of His garment, you'll be made whole and experience the peace of God in your storm. Touching the garment of Christ means believing what He says He will do, and who He says He is to you. It involves confessing God's Word and promises over your life and speaking them into your issues, until change comes. Faith, obedience, total surrender and submission are paramount.

Like this woman with no name, we need to have faith in God and not in the laws of men. Be obedient to the Word of God, rather than to what your situation is telling you. Surrender to God and not your circumstances and issues. This will strengthen you to press through the barriers before you and take possession of what Christ has already accomplished on your behalf. The woman no longer had faith in what the law said concerning her issue of blood, and was no longer subject to the law, because Christ offered her something that the law could not—freedom from her issue. She believed Jesus above the law.

Jesus didn't treat the woman without a name the way society treated her. He was by no means offended by her bleeding. Why? Because unlike men, He saw His identity in her, regardless of her issue. God will not hide Himself from us as we face our issues, or when we become "defiled or unclean" as a result of life's issues. God reminds us, *For we do not have a High Priest who cannot sympathize with our weaknesses, but was in all points* tempted as *we are, yet* without sin (Hebrew 4:15 NKJV).

Jesus is touched by your issues and infirmities, and He empathizes with you. He understands your pain, isolation and need for love, healing, comfort, intimacy, peace and wholeness. In His life on earth, Jesus was hurt, abandoned by those He loved, wounded, chastised, bruised, broken, rejected, isolated and betrayed. That however, did not stop Him from pressing toward that which the Father God had set before Him. For the joy that the Father had set before Him, He took on the shame and endured the cross.

Your identity is in Christ and not in man. You can escape all your storms if you embrace your identity in Christ. Don't allow your issues to isolate you or tempt you to turn your back on the Lord or doubt Him. Don't allow them to cause you to give up on God or your destiny. You're never without hope; Christ is your Help and your Hope. Begin to see yourself as Christ sees you. This will empower you to come out of hiding and isolation and press through until you break through.

Go to Jesus with your shame and issues, as He's already been through it all for your sake and mine. Jesus has already paid the price for the issue you're going through. All that is required of you is to go to Him for that which He's already paid. Refuse to let any issue keep you from receiving that which is rightfully yours in Christ. Refuse to let your identity be suffocated by what others have done to make you feel unworthy.

The woman experienced an intimate moment in the presence of the Lord, when she touched Him, and His power flowed through her trembling body, resulting in her healing. In that instant, she knew that she'd been delivered. Death was reversed, the blood dried up, and intimacy was restored. Twelve years of pain, doctors and medicine had ended. Twelve years of disappointment and isolation were over. The woman with an issue of blood now had a new identity as "daughter." In that moment, Jesus affirmed her womanhood, her beauty and the reason for which she was created—intimacy.

Beloved, you too are created for intimacy with God, and He is about to restore your womanhood or your manhood. In the Levitical law men were also deemed as unclean when the Lord spoke to Moses and Aaron saying, *"Speak to the children of Israel, and say to them: 'When any man has a discharge from his body, his discharge is unclean. And this shall be his uncleanness in regard to his discharge—whether his body runs with his discharge, or his body is stopped up by his discharge, it is his uncleanness" (Leviticus 51:2-3 NKJV).*

This illustration might refer to a woman; however, men do have issues that cause them to be unclean, and they are by no means exempted from pain, suffering, isolation or rejection. Whoever you are, God is more than able to end the issues in your life. As you continue to seek and press toward that intimate contact with Him, His power will be released into your life not only to heal you, but make you whole, granting you peace on every side. I remember a chorus to a song we used to sing that says,

Reach out and touch the Lord as He passes by.
You'll find He's not too busy to hear your heart's cry.
He's passing by this moment your need to supply.
Reach out and touch the Lord as He passes by.
Bill Harmon

Jesus is always beside us, always passing by. In fact, His Spirit resides inside us. All we need to do is reach out to Him as He is reaching out to us by His Word and presence. Don't give up; your solution is imminent.

CHAPTER FOUR

Against All Odds

The scriptures read,

Then Jesus entered and passed through Jericho. *Now behold, there was* a man named Zacchaeus who was a chief tax collector, and he was rich. *And he sought to see who Jesus was, but could not because of the crowd, for he was of short stature. So he ran ahead and climbed up into a sycamore tree to see Him, for He was going to pass that way. And when Jesus came to the place, He looked up and saw him, and said to him, "Zacchaeus, make haste and come down, for today I must stay at your house." So he made haste and came down, and received Him joyfully. But when they saw it,* they all complained, saying, "He has gone to be a guest with a man who is a sinner." *Then Zacchaeus stood and said to the Lord, "Look, Lord, I give half of my goods to the poor; and if I have taken anything from anyone by false accusation, I restore fourfold."*

And Jesus said to him, "Today salvation has come to this house, because he also is a son of Abraham; for the Son of Man has come to seek and to save that which was lost" (Luke 19:1–10).

Jesus is continually moving into the different arenas of our lives. He is constantly passing by and constantly with us. There is a chorus that says,

Jesus is passing this way, this way, this way;
Jesus is passing is passing this way; He's passing this way right now.

Right now, and right where you are, and what you're going through—Jesus is there and is passing by, ready to turn aside to minister to your need.

At one point, Jesus arrived in the city of Jericho, which was noted for an abundance of honey, cyprus, balsam and other aromatic plants and fragrances. Jesus always enters a place that carries a sweet-smelling fragrance. Because of the diverse challenges we face, our lives might not smell of sweet fragrances. However, God who turns bitter water sweet, can also smell His fragrance (the one inside us where He resides) where we cannot.

At the place where we smell a stench of death, as in the case of Lazarus in John 11, Jesus smells the aroma of life. In times of sickness, He senses healing and in moments of turmoil, He senses a great calm. Wherever His presence goes He carries the aroma of life, healing and blessings, whether we can identify them or not.

In the city of Jericho, there was a man named Zacchaeus, who, though residing in a pleasant place, was not without issues. He was a chief tax collector and a very wealthy man, but he wasn't immune to the cares of life. His name means pure and innocent. However, he never lived up to the true identity of his name. This sometimes happens to us; we might find ourselves facing a challenge that prevents us from living out our true identity in Christ.

That unrest caused him to seek after Jesus, who was, at that time, passing by. Can we truly say that during our trials, we're intentional in seeking after Jesus? Zacchaeus must have known that what he lacked, was not available from human beings. It goes without saying, that though we live in pleasant places, things are lacking that only Jesus and the love of God can fill.

The Psalmist wrote, *give us help from trouble, for the help of man is useless (Psalm 60:11 NKJV)*. In a time of desperation and curiosity, Zacchaeus sought after Jesus to find answers to questions he pondered in his heart. You might be in a somewhat pleasant place—but even there, it's not without difficulties, which is why it's paramount to seek Him and His Word at such times.

In seeking after Jesus, Zacchaeus faced obstacles because of the massive crowd and the fact that he was short in stature. Zacchaeus then ran ahead and climbed up into a sycamore tree to see Him, for Jesus was approaching the place where Zacchaeus was. Knowing that, Zacchaeus decided that, against all odds, he had to see Jesus.

Had Zacchaeus focused on his short stature, the crowd, what he was going through, or what people thought of him, he wouldn't have noticed the tree that he climbed to see Jesus. If he'd concentrated on his reputation as a greedy tax collector and thief, he wouldn't have discovered the means of catching the attention of Jesus—the tree.

We can be so focused on our storms that we're blind to the one thing God wants to us to use to "catch His attention." We can be so busy looking at our storms that we can't see the "tree"—our vantage point.

Often times we think we need something monumental to happen—a great deliverance, or a great breakthrough, before we can meet with the Lord and dine with Him in love. You might think you have to encounter something supernatural before you can see that God is truly working things out for your good. Many don't think they've met the prerequisites, all because their beginnings were small.

I encourage you to look for that "tree" –that seemingly insignificant thing that you need to "climb" in order to step into agreement with the Lord and His will. Look for the "tree" that will propel you to the next level and take you a step closer to greatness, delivering you from your issues. Against all odds, there's one thing that you need to do: press toward the place of divine encounter and turnaround. Like the woman with the issue of blood—against all odds, push through to where you can touch Him; in the end, it will result in your salvation and deliverance.

The "tree" is usually right before our eyes and at times we see it, but we despise it because we think others might laugh at or ridicule us. Whatever you need to do to get closer to Jesus Christ, do it. If you sincerely want to see the manifestation of Christ in your life, you'll break through barriers to encounter Him, no matter what it costs you. He is your only help in your time of trouble. There was once a man who was blind. The Bible said of Him,

Now they came to Jericho. As He went out of Jericho with His disciples and a great multitude, blind Bartimaeus, the son of Timaeus, sat by the road begging. And when he heard that it was Jesus of Nazareth, he began to cry out and say, "Jesus, Son of David, have mercy on me!"

Then many warned him to be quiet; but he cried out all the more, "Son of David, have mercy on me!"

So Jesus stood still and commanded him to be called.

Then they called the blind man, saying to him, "Be of good cheer. Rise, He is calling you."

And throwing aside his garment, he rose and came to Jesus.

So Jesus answered and said to him, "What do you want Me to do for you?"

The blind man said to Him, "Rabboni, that I may receive my sight."

Then Jesus said to him, "Go your way; your faith has made you well." And immediately he received his sight and followed Jesus on the road (Mark 10:46-52 NKJV).

Once again Jesus went to Jericho, to release His aroma into the life of one who desperately needed Him. Blind Bartimaeus was begging at the roadside as Jesus walked by. When he sensed that Jesus was passing by, he cried out for salvation and deliverance. Many in the crowd told him to shut up, however, against all odds he cried out even louder, until he captured the attention of Jesus. In spite of the negative attention of the crowd, he pressed through. There is no diplomacy in desperation. If you desperately desire to be free from your trials, then go beyond the status quo; despise the shame and ignore the opinions of others. The important thing is that Jesus is passing by, so it's your moment to press in and let His aroma fill your life once more. What is of importance is that Jesus is passing by and you need His aroma to fill your life. You need Him to touch you, make you whole and grant you peace, by reason of your faith.

Aware that his appointed time of healing and deliverance had come, blind Bartimaeus threw off his garment and went to Jesus for a brand-new identity. He shed his cloak, leaving behind the shame and ridicule of men, got rid of his old label, and went away an entirely different person. He knew Jesus was about to change his life and he got himself ready for that change by casting off the old garment that identified who he was—a beggar. Are you truly ready for the change that God is bringing your way? Then be like Zacchaeus and Blind Bartimaeus; "climb the tree" and cry out aloud to the Lord of your salvation, against all odds.

Whilst Zacchaeus was in the tree, Jesus *looked up and saw him, and said to him, "Zacchaeus, make haste and come down, for today I must stay at your house." So he made haste and came down, and received Him joyfully.* Although the tree was a help to Zacchaeus', when he was in that tree and caught Jesus' attention, He quickly told him to come down from the tree. Not only did Jesus tell Zacchaeus to come down, but to *"make haste."* Though the tree was his access point, he wasn't meant to remain there and become a mere spectator, although that was his intention when he climbed that tree. "He *sought to see who Jesus was"* and couldn't even imagine eating or fellowshipping with Him.

Zacchaeus wasn't seeking to know Christ or to become personally acquainted with Him. And while he may have had needs of his own, he may've been drawn to the miracles, for which He was widely known. Or maybe he wanted to hear Him teach the crowd, while he was in the tree. Jesus had a greater plan for Zacchaeus, wanting to move him from a place of seeing, to a place of knowing Him personally.

Jesus told him, "Come down from the tree now that you have caught my attention. Make haste." Zacchaeus was so desperate to see Jesus that he climbed a tree. It might sound controversial, but when you see Jesus coming, don't stay there! He's beckoning you to come down from that place and enter the banqueting hall of the King of kings. Come from that place and move to a place of fellowship and intimacy with the Lord, your Salvation and Saviour.

Often times we encounter Christ during a trial. We get to a desperate place in our lives when we realize that human beings can't help us anymore, and the solutions we seek, the refuge and strength we need are far beyond the capacity of men. We then turn to Jesus from that place of desperation, which then becomes the "tree" from which we search for the Jesus we've heard so much about. We start to cry out to God from within the storm, and we look to see Him coming our way.

Let me reiterate the truth, that God doesn't cause bad things to happen to us. However, He will allow them to happen to accomplish His will and purpose. He will allow them in order to catch our attention, which He's been seeking for so long. With nowhere to go and no one else to turn to, we then begin to cry out to Jesus and seek after Him, from within our storms. At some stage our issues will compel us to seek Jesus when all else fails.

Just as the desperate situation with the tree and the roadside became for Zaccheus and Blind Bartimaeus, those kinds of situations become our stepping stones to Jesus. In response to seeing Jesus, Bartimaeus got up and cast his garment aside. And Jesus told Zaccheus to, "come down." In like manner, when we finally meet Jesus, He doesn't want us to stay in that place anymore. He expects us to move from the place of hurt and rejection to the place of intimacy with Him and to the place of knowing Him. It's time to get up from the "roadside" and follow after Christ.

Trials and storms are much like trees to which we run for help; however, once we meet Jesus, we have to come out of the storm, where we can then access His divine ability to rescue us from the storm and break the hold of that which caused us to be in the storm in the first place. We must not despise the "tree", "the roadside" or the trials and challenges, but once we find Him, we must follow Him to the place where we can then triumph. Whether in the tree top or by the roadside, in the trial, you're still a victim. Once you come down from that "tree" and get up from the "roadside", you're on your way to becoming a true victor in Christ Jesus.

Though the tree was to Zacchaeus' advantage, had he remained there, it would've become an obstacle to his salvation. Obstacles like trees are fortifications which we can use to our advantage to get closer to the Lord. However, don't allow obstacles to become hindrances that prevent you from following passionately after Christ. The tree served its purpose. Likewise, the stormy winds, issues, trials and temptations we experience serve their purpose, but we must let go of them when Jesus makes Himself known to us. We cannot encounter Christ, yet remain the same by choosing to hold on to the things that are destroying our lives.

When you seek after Jesus and He reveals Himself to you in the midst of the storm, don't hold on to bitterness and unforgiveness. Forgive those who offended or abused you in any way. In the end, when you ask the Lord to intervene in your trials, you must let go and let Him lead you into healing and complete recovery.

If Zacchaeus had remained in the tree top, he would've seen Jesus the Saviour, yet he wouldn't have encountered His salvation. Making haste to come down from the tree, Zacchaeus not only saw and met the Saviour; he received the salvation message and intimacy with God. Jesus said to Zacchaeus, *"Today salvation has come to this house, because he also is a son of Abraham; for the Son of Man has come to seek and to save that which was lost."* Though Zacchaeus had only come for a glimpse of Jesus, Jesus went further—both to seek and save the lost. He came to seek and save those who are troubled by life's storms. He came both to reveal Himself as Saviour and to minister His salvation to all who will receive Him.

Jesus Himself was placed on the cross, a type of tree. However, He came down or was brought down, buried and rose again on the third day according to the Holy Scriptures. As a result, salvation and abundant life have been made available to all who believe on Him, receive Him and confess Him as Lord and Saviour. The cross or "tree" drew Jesus closer to His divine purpose of bringing salvation to mankind. Though Jesus died on the "tree", His purpose as both our Saviour and Salvation was completely manifest when He was brought down from the cross, buried and rose again.

Jesus had to come down from the cross— "the tree", in the same way that Zacchaeus could not stay in the tree. There was a divine principle and mystery in what Jesus asked Zacchaeus to do in coming down from the tree. On coming down from the tree Zacchaeus as it were, died to sin and received the life of God. He said to Jesus, *"Look, Lord, I give half of my goods to the poor; and if I have taken anything from anyone by false accusation, I restore fourfold."* This was a statement of confession and repentance which brought Zacchaeus the salvation of the Saviour. Jesus took our sin, nailed it to the cross, was buried and rose on the third day in the fullness of resurrection power, glory and the life of God. Jesus is not only the Saviour of the world; He is the Resurrection and the Life. This power of God's salvation was made available to you and me through repentance of our sins and accepting Jesus as Lord and Saviour just as Zacchaeus did. I believe this is one of the mysteries of the cross that lies in the story of Zacchaeus receiving the salvation of Jesus Christ.

When Zacchaeus made haste and came down from the tree, the crowd complained, saying, *"He has gone to be a guest with a man who is a sinner."* I'm sure Zacchaeus heard this, but it didn't bother him at all. Don't be bothered by the words of others when you have a chance to sit at the dinner table with Christ. Don't be bothered by the words of men when you decide to accept the invitation to Jesus' salvation. He alone is the One who died for you.

Refuse to allow anyone or anything to keep you up in the tree, always a spectator but never a recipient of God's love, mercy and grace. Refuse to remain a spiritual or physical beggar, always depending on others, when God is willing to activate His power of salvation in your life. All you need to do is go directly to Him. People will not always be able to rescue you and even if they can, He may prevent it, in order to prove His power and love in a personal way just for you.

When Jesus finds you, or passes by you and you encounter Him in this trial, follow Him wholeheartedly, for He has a meal prepared for you. When desperate times call for desperate measures, let your desperation move you to seek Him with all your heart—the only One who can save and deliver you. In the belly of a whale, in a desperate time of his life while running away from the assignment of God; Jonah recalled this to mind when he said,

"But I will sacrifice to You
With the voice of thanksgiving;
I will pay what I have vowed.
Salvation is of the LORD" (Jonah 2:9 NKJV).

The belly of the whale was the "tree top" or place of desperation from which Jonah not only recalled that salvation is of the Lord, but also sought the God of His salvation. In the belly of the fish, he offered thanksgiving and decided to honour his vow to the Lord. The Lord then spoke to the fish, and it vomited Jonah onto dry land.

Like Jonah, you might be trapped, in a seemingly impossible situation. If that describes you, I encourage you to remember that salvation is of the Lord, who is your Salvation. Only Jesus can save you in desperate times. "Climb a tree" if you must, cry out loudly to God and go beyond the ordinary. But keep this in mind: "I'm looking for Jesus and seeking after Him from the height of desperation." When He comes to your rescue, leave that "tree top" and rush to get out of that situation. Just as it was for Jonah, getting out of that tree requires you to simply vow to do what the Lord has asked you to do, because His perfect will is the only safe place to abide.

Zacchaeus knew that the only thing that mattered was what Jesus said and did, and you and I should know this too. Some people will wish you to remain where you are, desperate and deteriorating, but God wants you to be made whole and be at perfect peace. While many still seek after Christ, many are still dying in their desperation, which is why you can't remain in the tree top. Come down and let God use you to be His instrument of salvation. Others are depending on you to come down from where you are, and to make haste in doing so.

Your ministry is no longer in the tree top; it's on the ground, preaching salvation to the lost and being a witness of what God has done in your life. Many are waiting on you to tell them about the One who lovingly offered His hand of salvation to you. The Bible tells us,

The people who sat in darkness have seen a great light,
And upon those who sat in the region and shadow of death
Light has dawned" (Matthew 4:16 NKJV).

The operative word here is "sat." When light has come in your darkness, move, change your abode and dwell with Christ and in Christ—the Light of the world.

As Christians, we've already caught the attention of Christ and obtained His salvation. The question remains, are we still sitting in the tree top? Are we allowing the crowd, storms and trials to cause us to be mere spectators? From the crowd Zacchaeus pushed his way up the tree. From the roadside the beggar made his way to Jesus. Where are you at this moment? Are you even trying to make an effort to get away from that which hinders you from living your best life in God? For all you know God has allowed this trial to draw you toward Him and the blessings He has in store for you.

One day Jesus met a Samaritan woman at a well. She had many issues that isolated her, which meant she could only go to the well during the hottest time of the day, when no one was around to see her because of the shame she bore (See John 4). After Christ ministered to her at the well, she received the gospel with great joy, and abandoned everything to run into the city shouting, *"Come see a man, who told me all things I ever did. Could this be the Christ?" (John 4:29, NKJV)*. Her point of desperation was the well, and to get there she had to push beyond society's opinions, because of her questionable reputation.

However, at the well, Jesus found her in her desperation and changed both her story and her destiny. She quickly gave up everything and ran to declare that she had found the Christ—the One who changed her life forever! We'll all see Jesus from either the crowd like the woman with the issue of blood, from the tree top, from the roadside or by the "wells" of our lives—the places we go when no one is around, simply because we are ashamed of who and where we are. One thing for sure, the salvation of God is beyond the crowd, the roadside, the tree top and the well.

In the end, the woman at the well won souls to Christ when she shifted location and left her desperation behind. She became an evangelist as soon as she left the well and went into the city against all odds. Remember, Jesus had changed her story, but the people of the city knew nothing of that, yet she went into the city and was no longer afraid to been seen, bothered by the opinions of others. All she knew was that she was no longer in darkness, and she took the light of God into her community.

You might be in a storm, but Jesus will change you and your story if you let Him. When He does, don't be afraid to let it be known to the world, as it's for the salvation and deliverance of others, including those who thought nothing good of you. When you're fully persuaded that Jesus has met you by your "well" and changed you, let no one tell you otherwise. Refuse to remain in darkness and let His light shine through you. Push your way out of the storm! Push your way out of bondage and limitations! Your salvation and deliverance is beyond the storms. Your assignment is beyond the well and beyond your current challenge.

Jesus is still in the business of seeking and saving the lost. He's still seeking to save our lost families and loves ones. Jesus is the Harvester of souls, and the Holy Spirit is the Spirit of that harvest. Your storm is not meant to destroy you, but to empower you by the grace, power, and the Word and Spirit of God, you'll fulfil your divine assignment. Push toward the Master, press against the obstacles that prevent you from an encounter with God that will bring about a change in your life and the destinies of others.

God wants to bring you out of trouble, so push against the barriers. Refuse to watch others enjoy the joy of the Lord's salvation while you remain bound in your trials. Make up your mind that you'll obtain the salvation of Christ against all odds, and in doing so, you'll take the joy, peace and salvation of Christ into your neighbourhood, to your family, friends and loved ones and even the strangers who have no idea how to extricate themselves from desperate situations.

You are the God's instrument of light in this world, and nothing will dim your light, once you break through every limitation. Take a step of faith toward the Saviour who is too faithful to fail you. Move from victim to victor in Christ Jesus. Remind yourself, *"I can do all things through Christ who strengthens me" (Philippians 4:13)*. All things include making only wise decisions that glorify and please God. The Holy Spirit in us is still able to empower us to live an abundant life in Christ. We have what it takes to pray and declare our way out of every storm, and destroy the devices and schemes of the enemy. You aren't helpless in this trial—you have the indwelling of the Holy Spirit to see you through them all, to the glory of God!

God doesn't just want you to dwell in a pleasant place; He wants pleasantness to be found within you. God wants an atmosphere of peace, joy and righteousness to surround you. When you dwell in a pleasant place and pleasantness is found within you, then you'll experience the fruitfulness and prosperity of God in every area of your life. In the words of the Shulamite to her beloved,

"Behold, you are handsome, my beloved!
Yes, pleasant!
Also our bed is green" (Songs of Solomon 1:15 NKJV).

Beauty can be all around us, but even better than beauty is pleasantness. Pleasantness in and around us will keep our intimacy with God fresh, green, fruitful and productive. May you not only dwell in a pleasant place like Jericho, but may pleasantness be found inside you, that you might be productive and flourish in Him against all odds.

Chapter Five

When All You Get Is Crumbs

As we go through storms, we might expect our deliverance to come in a way greater than the storms, perhaps moving in a dramatic way, that will bring an immediate resolution to the problem. The Bible refers to one handmaiden who might have had such great expectations, calling her "a woman of Canaan", who sought Jesus in great desperation, concerning a matter of life and death.

In Matthew 15:21-28 NKJV we read,

Then Jesus went out from there and departed to the region of Tyre and Sidon. And behold, a woman of Canaan came from that region and cried out to Him, saying, "Have mercy on me, O Lord, Son of David! My daughter is severely demon-possessed."
But He answered her not a word.
And His disciples came and urged Him, saying, "Send her away, for she cries out after us."
But He answered and said, "I was not sent except to the lost sheep of the house of Israel."
Then she came and worshiped Him, saying, "Lord, help me!"

But He answered and said, "It is not good to take the children's bread and throw it to the little dogs."
And she said, "Yes, Lord, yet even the little dogs eat the crumbs which fall from their masters' table."
Then Jesus answered and said to her, "O woman, great is your faith! Let it be to you as you desire." And her daughter was healed from that very hour.

This woman was a descendant of the Canaanites and was not a Jew but a Gentile, and was considered unworthy of Jesus' blessing. When she approached Christ, she addressed Him as the Son of David. He didn't respond to her because that title was only used by the Jews when speaking of the Messiah. As a Gentile she had no right to approach Him that way, which is why He didn't respond to her. Jesus was not being cruel but rather testing her faith.

The disciples also considered this Gentile woman to be a nuisance, even asking Jesus to send her away. In other words, they asked the Lord to give her what she desired, that she might leave them alone, as she was not only an uninvited guest, but very unwelcome. Jesus responded that He hadn't been sent to this Gentile but to God's chosen people—the nation of Israel.

Still the woman did not give up. *Then she came and worshiped Him, saying, "Lord, help me!"*
But He answered and said, "It is not good to take the children's bread and throw it to the little dogs."
And she said, "Yes, Lord, yet even the little dogs eat the crumbs which fall from their masters' table." A few things are notable here, and one is the woman's approach. As previously mentioned, she first approached Jesus addressing Him as Son of David, a title that got no response from Him, because, as a Gentile, she had no right to use that title. Then she changed her approach and worshipped Him—this time addressing Him as Lord.

Addressing Jesus as Lord commanded a response from Jesus. She might not have been one of God's chosen people, but as one of His creation, calling Him Lord entitled her to His attention. Though Jesus was first sent to the nation of Israel, He also knew that His mandate when fulfilled, would extend salvation to both Jews and Gentiles. He knew His death would one day bring near, those who were once a far off like this Gentile woman.

Paul wrote, *Or is He* the God of the Jews only? *Is He* not also the God of the Gentiles? Yes, of the Gentiles also, (Romans 3:29 *NKJV)*. There is a lesson for us to learn here. When the woman didn't get a response with her first approach, she tried a different approach that yielded results. Jesus once said, *"And in that day you will ask Me nothing. Most assuredly, I say to you, whatever you ask the Father in My name He will give to you. Until now you have asked nothing in My name. Ask, and you will receive, that your joy may be full" (John 16:23-24 NKJV)*. Have you ever prayed during your storms and it appeared as though the Lord wasn't responding to your petitions? Maybe, like the woman whose first approach was wrong, our approach in prayer is also sometimes wrong, and heaven will be silent. Jesus said, *"Until now you have asked nothing in My name."* Many times, when we approach the Lord in prayer, truly we have asked amiss. Praying amiss is the same as asking the Lord nothing.

Sometimes we pray for our own desires and not His. We go to the Lord with our agenda, and not God's agenda, or we approach Him with wrong motives and wrong desires. James said, *"You ask and do not receive, because you ask amiss, that you may spend it on your pleasures" (James 4:3 NKJV)*. Are we approaching God with selfish desires in our hearts? Yes, you want the storms to cease, but what is your motive in prayer? Why are you praying for that need in your life? Why are you praying that kind of prayer?

When the woman didn't get a response because she asked amiss, she chose an approach that eventually favoured her cause. She asked in accordance to the will of the Lord Jesus. Maybe God appears silent in the midst of the storm because our approach in prayer is wrong. Prayer must be according to the will of God, and not based on our selfish desires. Prayer must be led by the One who knows the mind and will of God for our lives—that is the Holy Spirit!

Whether we believe it or not, vain repetitions don't attract the attention of the Lord. Jesus said, *"When you pray, do not use vain repetitions as the heathens do. For they think that they will be heard for their many words."* Repeating empty, useless words and phrases in prayer will not cause the Lord to hear us. Prayer should not contain formulaic phrases. Let your prayers be led by the Spirit and based upon the words and promises of God, steered toward the fulfilment of the will and purpose of God. Allow the Spirit of God to pray the will and desires of the Lord through you, for that will bring about the corresponding blessings and deliverance you seek.

When the woman finally got it right, the response of Jesus appeared somewhat harsh. He said, *"It is not good to take the children's bread and throw it* to the little dogs." How many of us would have given up, cursed the Lord, cursed His servants, and given in to our fate. Jesus did not respond to her. Instead, He spoke over her letting her know He was not sent to her. Basically, her problem was not His concern. At that point, He blatantly addressed her as a dog. Jesus told her He was not about to waste the grace and favour He had come to bestow upon God's chosen people on anyone else, nor count it as worthless by having her be a partaker. Wow! I'm sure many of us would have been fuming by then!

The woman was persistent and persevered, refusing to be offended at His words. She was desperate to see the demon cast out of her child, to see a change in her situation, and was prepared to do whatever it took to see it happen. She knew that though she was unworthy, no man but Jesus could help. The Saviour was right in front of her, and against all odds, she wasn't leaving without her breakthrough.

This Gentile woman was willing to put up with anything in order to see her baby girl whole again. What about us? Today, Christians are easily offended by what God did for others and didn't do for them. Others are offended by what they think God has allowed to happen to them. And many are offended because they suffered at the hands of others. If others don't respond the way we expect them to, we're offended.

Offense is one of the major weapons the devil uses to delay and block our blessings. This woman refused to be offended. A boisterous storm was blowing all around her, and she was desperate for a resolution. She was by no means moved by the comments of Jesus, His disciples or anyone who knew she was a Gentile and undeserving of the deliverance and salvation she sought. She kept her focus and fixed her gaze on the one that held the key to her breakthrough, and never allowed the wind to distract her. In the end, she remained intentional in what she was about.

What about you this very minute? Are you allowing offense to stop you from seeking the deliverance you so desire? Are you allowing pride to keep you a casualty of stormy winds? Are you angry with God and others? There are times when God will use others to deliver you from the trials and storms. He might choose to use someone that is naturally arrogant; nonetheless, at times we have to swallow our pride and allow the Lord to use them to manifest His will in our lives. God will also allow this situation to strip us of unwanted character traits and mature us in His character.

Without offense in her heart, the woman of Canaan responded, *"Yes, Lord, yet even the little dogs eat the crumbs which fall from their masters' table."* What courage and strength! Nothing was an obstacle to this Gentile woman. She agreed that she wasn't worthy of the healing she sought for her child, "Nonetheless, do it for one of your creatures." This woman stood in great faith and humility. King Solomon wrote, *I returned and saw under the sun that—*

The race is not for the swift,
Nor the battle to the strong,
Nor bread to the wise,
Nor riches to men of understanding,
Nor favour to men of skill;
But time and chance happen to them all (Ecclesiastes 9:11 NKJV).

This woman must have known that swiftness, strength, wisdom, understanding and skills are good, but they don't necessarily guarantee the blessings, breakthrough or deliverance we seek. She must've known that the same denominators are available to all: time and chance, and both were right in front of her. She knew that Jesus was passing her way, and it was the right time for her daughter's deliverance. She knew that, though by law she was disqualified, underserving of what she asked—it was her opportunity, to obtain salvation for her demon-possessed child, and against all odds she was seizing the moment at all cost.

The common denominators we all share are time and chance. Our deliverance demands that we know and cooperate with God's timing that will bring about the salvation and deliverance we seek. God has appointed His time of deliverance and presents us with many opportunities. Sadly, many of us don't recognize His timing, and even when we do, we fail to take advantage in the moment. We can even allow obstacles to create in us a spirit of procrastination.

We settle for the sentences pronounced on us and disregard the timing and opportunities the Lord presents to us for freedom.

Many people experience cyclical fluctuations, simply because they fail to grasp hold of God's timing and opportunities. We need to know that God has placed an opportunity before us, no matter how small it appears. We need to know when to seize the moment and not allow a spirit of delay to rob us of our blessings. Learn to work with God; when He speaks, respond accordingly and then do just what He tells you to do. Break the spirit of delay and procrastination off your life!

Like the Canaanite woman, would you be willing to accept crumbs? Sometimes when facing trials, God might not give us what we think we deserve; rather, He gives us just what we need to escape the storms. The woman understood the power of both the bread and the crumbs. She understood that the crumbs were made up of exactly the same ingredients as the bread. It carried the same potency and efficacy as an entire loaf of bread. In fact, she was bright enough to realize she would be getting the whole loaf, in the end.

She knew that they might need a whole loaf of bread to satisfy their needs, however, all she needed were the crumbs that came from the same Source and Supplier—Jesus Christ. There was a time in 2006-2007, when I was going through a storm. One day, whilst waiting for a ride to work I saw a young lady on a motor bike, who somehow caught my attention.

I remember watching her intently as she drove the roundabout, when suddenly she stopped in front of me. She looked at me and said with a slight Spanish accent, "Sister, Jesus loves you." Lost in a quandary I thought to myself, "What just happened?" For a split second, I looked momentarily at the ground, but when I looked up to meet her gaze, she was nowhere to be seen. This woman would have had to ride at least a short distance before disappearing from sight; to me it was very strange.

I thought to myself, "Was she an angel?" I was baffled and have not forgotten that encounter to this day! It seemed like I got crumbs from God that day when she said, "Sister, Jesus loves you." Jesus loves you? Can you imagine! I thought, "With all I'm going through, that was all the Lord said to me?" As you can imagine, I was dissatisfied with so little, as if I didn't know Jesus loved me. I expected to be delivered in a big way if God was sending His messenger to me. At the time, I thought the phrase, "Jesus loves you" couldn't possibly solve my problems. I needed an exceedingly, abundantly, far above and far beyond miracle, and I needed it like yesterday!

God however, knew that all I needed then were those few words, "Jesus loves you." How great and unconditional is the love of God— the love that compelled Him to give His only begotten Son to die for us, that we might be delivered out of sin and bondage, and have hope for everlasting life! God is not always in the big, extravagant and exciting things. The Bible reminds us of the Prophet Elijah's encounter with God when it reads,

Then He said, "Go out, and stand on the mountain before the Lord." And behold, the Lord passed by, and a great and strong wind tore into the mountains and broke the rocks in pieces before the Lord, but the Lord was not in the wind; and after the wind an earthquake, but the Lord was not in the earthquake; and after the earthquake a fire, but the Lord was not in the fire; and after the fire a still small voice (1Kings 19:11-12 NKJV).

God spoke to His servant not in a dramatic and extravagant way, but in a still small voice. As we go through the storms, we need to know that God doesn't need to shout to free us from our trials. In stillness and quietness, He'll release a command that will liberate us from it all.

The woman, an outcast and a Gentile, accepted that the bread was for the Jews, God's chosen people; nonetheless, she was satisfied to have the crumbs that fell from the Master's table. She knew that even a little from the Lord carried His powerful authority, power and dominion to rebuke that which was tormenting her child. And it was enough to make her child well again.

When He saw the determination, courage, strength, and gratitude for the crumbs, but even more importantly, the faith of this Gentile woman, He said to her, *"O woman, great is your faith! Let it be to you as you desire."* And her daughter was healed from that very hour. The woman mixed the crumbs with faith and not only was her child healed, but Jesus commended her for her faith. What about you and me? What are you going through that you think requires a great miracle from the Lord? Are we accepting the "little" we're being offered by the Lord? Can our faith in the little be commended before the Lord?

If you knew the potency and power of God's Word, you would be fully persuaded that no matter how few words of God you've received—those few words carry great miracles and blessings. You might be going through a distressing trial this very minute. God might send you a word by his messenger saying, "God bless you." Or, "Jesus loves you." You might be seeking God fervently in prayer, and the only voice you can hear, is a still small voice saying, "Fear not, I am with you." Can you combine those few words with faith, to bring about the deliverance you seek? Or, do you think that God hasn't said enough or that His few words are ineffective to tame your storms?

The bread, wind, earthquake and fire all have their places, but the crumbs have their place as well. I know that it was, it is and it always will be the love of God that brings me through every storm. No matter the challenges I encounter, may I always remember that Jesus loves me. I know that because He loves me, He'll always see me through. Because Jesus loves me, He'll be faithful to lead, guide and protect me through the storms. These are "crumbs" that I'll never take for granted.

God's solutions to our issues and challenges are sometimes right before our eyes, but we don't see them because they seem small or ineffective. We might think God can't use simple methods to deliver us. Moses delivered God's people out of many years of slavery, torture and torment, by means of a simple rod, a piece of stick *(Exodus 4:1-17)*. This rod or shepherd's staff or stick, carried the power of the Almighty God to do signs, wonders and miracles! The apostle Paul puts it this way,

But God has chosen the foolish things of the world to put to shame the wise, and God has chosen the weak things of the world to put to shame the things which are mighty; and the base things of the world and the things which are despised God has chosen, and the things which are not, to bring to nothing the things that are (1Corinthians 1:27-28 NKJV).

Let's not be wise in our own eyes, thinking God can't use the simple things to deliver us. Let's not see as weak, the things that God has ordained to strengthen us and bring us out of our trials. Once it is of the Lord, it's mighty to save. In the hands of Almighty God, even weak things become mighty. We often miss our hour of God's visitation because we have closed our eyes, hearts, minds and spirits to that which God is saying and doing—thinking it's too simple to be of the Lord.

Messengers and helpers of God are rejected by many, simply because they don't look the way we expect them to. We can even reject our divine helpers because they aren't perfect. We might see a character trait we don't like, and we think "No way! God certainly cannot use this person to bless or deliver me!" Our ways are not the ways of God, nor are our thoughts His thoughts. *"For My thoughts are* not your thoughts, Nor *are* your ways My ways," says the LORD. *"For as* the heavens are higher than the earth, So are My ways higher than your ways, And My thoughts than your thoughts" *(Isaiah 55:8-9 NKJV).*

No matter how few the crumbs we see God using to deliver us, we must never despise them, because nothing is impossible with God, who does all things well. God is great and all that He does and says carry His greatness and power. When we can't imagine it happening, we must simply choose to trust God, knowing that He knows the end from the beginning. The Canaanite woman's daughter was made well from the hour she accepted the crumbs. She received a great miracle—far more than mere crumbs, because her faith was great! The greatness she received from Jesus was as a result of the little she was willing to accept by faith. Do not despise the crumbs.

GOD WANTS YOUR CRUMBS

During our challenging seasons when we think we lack enough to offer the Lord, He not only gives us "crumbs", but also desires us to use our "crumbs." There was once a woman who only had two mites to her name. Those two mites were said to worth less than a cent. She went into the temple and put them in the offering basket, while the rich were sowing enormous sums of money. This woman was widowed and no doubt, dwelling in great poverty. In fact, her two mites could even have been a loan from a neighbour or a friend.

I don't imagine that she ever had much, but she was grateful, believing that even those two mites were from the Lord. The Bible tells us that the eyes of Jesus were fixed on this poor widow as she brought her two mites to the offering as well as on others who brought their offerings. Jesus observed that many gave out of their abundance. After watching the woman put in her two mites, Jesus said, *"Assuredly, I say to you that this poor widow has put in more than all those who have given to the treasury; for they all put in out of their abundance, but she out of her poverty put in all that she had, her whole livelihood"* (verse 43-44 NKJV).

The woman appreciated God for the little He had given to her though she was impoverished and faced many challenges. She knew it was okay to give back to God the little she had, because, in His faithfulness He would continue to provide. And while God may not have delivered the woman out of her physical poverty, He had deposited within her a spiritual wealth that enabled her to continue worshipping Him, even in her poverty.

God might not take you out of your physical challenges and issues immediately or as quickly as you would like. However, even within that physical lack, know that He has deposited something in you that makes you spiritually rich. You might not have much to give to the Lord; you might not be able to pray to Him as skilfully as others do. You might not know much of His Word, and you might not be as spiritually wise or as mature as others. However, the little that you give out of the sincerity of your heart can move mountains on your behalf once you give it to God.

The widow's mites carried the power to activate the grace, goodness and favour of God in her life, and that was enough for her. Her two mites gave her the opportunity to be commended by the greatest Man who ever lived on the earth, and by the Supreme God and King who rules eternal. Her two mites and her giving were used by the Teacher Himself to teach many in ages past, in this age and the ages to come.

God might have given you what seems like "mites" in the hands of the widow. Why not use the little to glorify and worship the Lord even in the midst of trials and temptations? Why not use the little to bear testimony of God, and in turn, allow Him to make a testimony out of you, just as He did with the widow? Never think you have nothing to offer the Lord. Never think that what you have is not worth giving, and don't be ashamed if all you have to offer to God is a prayer that's no bigger than the "widow's mites."

I have asked the Lord for many things that would, in my opinion, have made my life more comfortable. Instead, He actually gave me the opposite of what I asked for. I have asked for a financial breakthrough; instead, He allowed someone to bless me with provisions. At that point, I thought to myself, "I don't need provisions, I need money!" Looking back, I now find this hilarious. God has always been my Provider, and when I thought I needed money, it's as though He said, "No! You need provisions!" To me the provisions were "widow's mites" in comparison to what I thought I needed.

Out of the provisions, I was able to bless others. Then I realised that the Word of God is true—He blesses us to become a blessing. It's as though the blessing wasn't just for me, but for someone else as well. Nothing is about us, but all about the will and purposes of the Lord. Don't be discouraged when whilst in the storm you made requests of the Lord, and all you seem to get is a "widow's mite." Use that "widow's mite" to continue serving Him and bless others too if you can. Say a little prayer for someone else, a loved one, and your family, and encourage others with what you know about the love and faithfulness of God. As you do so, God will make history out of your story as He did for that widow.

By reason of the challenges you're going through, your life might not seem like much of a story, but God will make history or "His Story" out of your story, as you continue to serve Him faithfully. The promise of God to us is, that if we are faithful in little, He will make us rulers over much. God will entrust us with little as He wants us to understand the value of the little He has given us. He also wants to see how we use and respond to the little, as well as how faithful we are in both receiving and giving back the little He has placed in our hands. Like the woman who accepted the crumbs, your "widow's mites" will deliver you from poverty and from the raging storms, if you accept and use it wisely.

CHAPTER SIX

Crossing to the Other Side

Before Jesus met with Jairus the ruler of the synagogue and the woman with the issue of blood, the Bible states, *"Now when Jesus has crossed over again by boat to the other side" (Mark 5:21a, NKJV).* Each time we're going to enter a new season in our lives, a "crossing over to the other side" takes place. Our crossing over is a place of change, divine shift and transition. Whenever Jesus crossed over to a place, changes took place, miracles and breakthroughs happened, deliverances occurred, and sight was restored to both the spiritually and physically blind. The sick were healed, the dead (both spiritually and physically) were raised, deaf ears (both spiritually and physically) were opened, the mute spoke, and the lame walked, and in the power of God's gospel, people heard the gospel.

Whenever Jesus crosses over to the other side He doesn't go alone; He takes His followers or disciples with Him. Matthew 9:1 tells us how Jesus got into a boat, crossed over and came to His own city. I'm sure He was not alone in the boat, but was accompanied by others. *Matthew 14:34* also spoke of when they had crossed over to the land of Gennesaret. The "they" the Bible was referring to was Jesus and His disciples.

When He did cross over, men recognized Him and multitudes began to follow Him. Jesus once crossed over and still crosses over into situations, lives and places. He still expects us as His disciples to cross over with Him. Paramount to note is that men recognized Jesus wherever He went *(See Matthew 14:35)*. This tells me that when we cross to the other side with Jesus, both people and the devil and his demons will recognize us. As in Joseph's case, we'll be noticed by both those who are good and those who are evil. Many saw the goodness of God and the good in him, while others looked at him with evil intent.

Our "crossing over" or transition will attract the attention of both friends and foes, as well as well-wishers and "evil-wishers." *Luke 8:22-25* says this:

Now it happened, on a certain day, that He got into a boat with His disciples. And He said to them, "Let us cross over to the other side of the lake." And they launched out. But as they sailed He fell asleep. And a windstorm came down on the lake, and they were filling with water, and were in jeopardy. And they came to Him and awoke Him, saying, "Master, Master, we are perishing!"

Then He arose and rebuked the wind and the raging of the water. And they ceased, and there was a calm. But He said to them, "Where is your faith?"

And they were afraid, and marvelled, saying to one another, "Who can this be? For He commands even the winds and water, and they obey Him!" (Luke 8:22-25 NKJV).

It's vital to note is that Jesus initiated the transition. He spearheaded this trip. It was Jesus' idea for them to, *"cross over to the other side of the lake."* This crossing over was the doing of the Lord and not of man. As they travelled, Jesus *fell asleep. And a windstorm came down on the lake, and their boat was filling with water,* and were in jeopardy. As they sailed and arrived at their appointed time of transition, the place of divine destiny, Jesus, the very Word of God, fell asleep in the boat.

When He fell asleep during a windstorm, the disciples were suddenly terrified, and as a result of their fear, their boat became vulnerable to the effects of the storm. Their lives were in jeopardy, because in their minds, the storm was gaining an advantage over them, until they began to panic. The question is: what caused them to begin to sink during their time of "crossing over?"

As they sailed, as they took a step toward God's divine call and purpose, setting the course that the Lord ordained, but when Jesus (the Word of God) fell asleep in their boat, they suddenly felt vulnerable, unaware that whether awake or asleep, He was still in control. Beloved, God is meant to be the Chief Orchestrator of our journeys, the One meant to direct and command the course changes we make. The Bible reminds us that the steps of a good or righteous man are ordered by the Lord, and He delights in his ways. The Psalmist reminds us that the Word of the Lord is a lamp to our feet and a light to our path *(See Psalms 37:23, Psalms 119:105).*

The fact is that while our steps are ordered by the Lord, who directs our paths as we commit our ways to Him, we're not exempt from life's storms. Those who choose to allow the Lord to direct their steps, will surely attract the attention of situations raging around us. However, one of the many reasons we succumb to our trials, sinking into deep water, is that we allow the Word of God to fall asleep inside us, instead of allowing it to motivate us to stand in faith, believing that He is still in control.

In our daily journey with God, we should refuse to let the Word of God go dormant, losing its power to protect us. When God is taking us to the "other side—a place of divine transformation, we ought to keep His Word and promises alive, active and hidden in our hearts, at the forefront of our minds, because we will need it as a weapon to defeat the storms that come against us.

If you begin to sink ever deeper into your troubles, first ask yourself this vital question, "Where is the Word of God?" As a matter of fact, if you need to ask yourself the question, God's Word is definitely asleep inside you. At times, we actually get comfortable in our situations, or are governed by our own will and emotions. And not only do we allow His Word to fall asleep inside us, but we wilfully reject it. If we allow our own desires to draw us in and motivate our behaviour, we often find that we pay a higher price than we wanted and could've avoided challenges had we only listened to and obeyed God's Word, taking it with us wherever we go.

King Solomon, the wisest man who ever lived, wrote that there is a way that seems right to man, but its end is the way of death *(Proverbs 14:12 NKJV)*. We become attractive to the spirit of death (not just physical but spiritual), and it pursues us all the more, especially when we travel a way that seems right in our eyes, and not the path that has been mapped out for us by the Lord Himself. Many succumb to various diabolical "windstorms" when somewhere along the path of transition, they forget that the Lord is in control.

Many men and women fall from their godly positions, simply because they begin to take credit for the blessings they received along the way. Everything becomes centred on them, and suddenly they find themselves sinking into the "deep waters" of greed, pride, arrogance and self-righteousness. At this time the gospel they preach becomes polluted, and it's no longer Christ who leads them; rather, they're led by their own fleshly desires. They inevitably become an attraction to diabolical winds that threaten their lives and ministries.

Beloved, when we start going as it were "underwater" in our walk with God and are faced with diverse "stormy winds", let's be quick to do a spiritual self-examination. If we can be true to ourselves, we'll realize that somewhere along our journey we have either rejected the Word of God, or allowed it to become dormant in our lives. Many of the "windstorms" we experience occur when we "cap" the Word of God, or forcibly put it to sleep inside us.

After Jesus fell asleep, the disciples began to cry out to the Word—Jesus Christ. Suddenly, they remembered He was in their boat, but asleep. *And they came to Him and awoke Him, saying, "Master, Master, we are perishing!"* The disciples told Jesus they were about to die! What a strange thing to say after awakening the Master over all—Jesus, the Word of God! What a faithless utterance after awakening the very Word of God.

Master! Master! was both a cry of fear and a cry of intercession. They thought they were doomed so they lifted their voices in prayer, petitioning the Word of God to arise. What is alarming about their petition, is that they cried out to the Lord, not to intervene, but rather to tell Him they were about to die! If their cry was for the purpose of escape, they should've asked Him to deliver them instead of declaring their doom. When raging waters begin to fill our lives, do we, like the disciples, tell God that the storm is greater than His Word—the God inside of us? That was exactly what the disciples did when they were driven by fear.

They told the Lord that the devil was succeeding in what he had orchestrated against them, and in the process, they told the devil he was winning. If you're going through trials, how would you respond to the Word of God inside you, the vessel of God? Have you written yourself off as doomed by life's "windstorms? Have you gone to God telling Him that His Word in you is impotent against your trials? Are you telling God that you, the conduit and bearer of His Word and promises—are facing a hopeless situation that cannot be resuscitated by His Word?

Believe it or not, this is exactly what we do when we go to God complaining about what the devil is doing. This is exactly what you do when you tell the Lord that things in your life, like your health, marriage, ministry, finances, children, or business are dead or dying (physically or spiritually). Looking at the storms and telling Him you're perishing is essentially saying that His Word is powerless and the devil has won.

Jesus was well aware that He was the Word of God, and that He wasn't helpless: *He arose and rebuked the wind and the raging of the water. And they ceased, and there was a calm. But He said to them, "Where is your faith?"* Jesus—the Word, arose and rebuked their unbelief. He did not arise and lament to God the Father that He and His disciples were about to perish. He arose; the Word of God personified arose and He rebuked the winds! With all authority given to Him by God the Father, the Word of God spoke to the wind and the water. He spoke with all authority against the devices of the enemy; *And they ceased, and there was a calm.*

All the that the devil was doing ceased immediately; the raging storm ceased, the trials ceased, the temptations and troubles ceased at the very command of the Word of God! Job and God were in conversation, when God stood in His identity as Creator and spoke to Job saying,

"Have you commanded the morning since your days began,
And caused the dawn to know its place,
That it might take hold of the ends of the earth,
And the wicked be shaken out of it?" (Job 38:12-13).

When the Word of God is resurrected within us, and when we call upon God's Word to activate it, we need to command the evil one to cease and desist. God's commanded Word causes the devil to know his place. His commanded words take control of the storms, forcing them to cease. Those wicked schemes are shaken out of our lives and out of our "vessels" when we issue a command and rebuke to the contrary winds and storms, using God's Word of authority.

When we speak the Word of God to negative circumstances, they know their place and cease their war and strife against us. Like the raging water that returned to its original state of calm, whatever the devil releases against us has to recede to its peaceful calm at the rebuke of God's Word. It takes the Word of God in us to shake the enemy's waters out of our boats. It takes the Word of God to chase out the wicked plans of the enemy in our lives.

Commanding your morning means speaking the Word of God into every area of your life. It's all about speaking forth the Word of God that will rebuke diabolic winds, waters, waves and currents, breaking cycles and cancelling evil decrees and diabolic utterances and bringing to pass the will of God for your life.

When the Word of God is declared or spoken forth, it takes hold of *the ends of the earth.* It doesn't matter where the devil and his cohorts are operating from; the Word of God travels faster than the speed of light and is able to neutralize the powers of darkness, irrespective of where they originate. Time and matter are no restrictions to God's Word! *In the beginning* (time) *God created the heavens and the earth* (matter). *The earth was without form and void* (space); *and darkness was on the face of the deep. And the Spirit of God was hovering over the face of the waters (Genesis 1:1-2 NKJV).* The Word of God carries God's divine power to gather your blessings from wherever they're located across the earth.

In the beginning was the Word, and the Word was with God, and the Word was God. He was in the beginning with God. All things were made through Him, and without Him, nothing was made that was made. In Him was life, and the life was the light of men (John 1:1-4 NKJV). The Word here is referring to Jesus Christ. All things were made by Him and through Him, both visible and invisible. Hence, when we speak God's Word it travels to the ends of the earth and creates, to the glory of God.

Just like Jesus spoke to the winds and they obeyed Him, so every element on earth—visible and invisible, is subject to God's Word and must obey it, when we speak it in faith. Let's refuse to undermine the Word of God, by crying as though Jesus (the Word of God) who created all things, is unable to address our storms. Though the winds might be boisterous, refrain from telling the Lord you're dying, or that your situation is hopeless.

Don't go to the Lord lamenting as though you're doomed to destruction and that you're without a Helper. He knows about your problems, and yes, you can tell Him what He already knows if you wish. Go ahead and pour out your heart to God, after all He is your Heavenly Father, and though as our Father He knows the dilemmas of His children, it doesn't mean He doesn't want to hear them from our lips. Confess your weaknesses and addictions to Him; however, remember to also speak His words and promises over your life as a counter petition to that which you're going through, until you see a great calm restored to your life. When it comes to talking to your Heavenly Father, share with hope, faith and confidence in His Word and promises for your life.

After the calm returned, Jesus asked His disciples, *"Where is your faith?"* I too must ask the question, in the midst of my trials: where is my faith? Is our faith in God's Word, or is it in what the devil is doing to us? At times we seem to believe more in what we see with our eyes than having faith in God's promises. We even discount what God's Word says the devil *cannot* do to us.

Job said, *"For the thing I greatly feared has come upon me, And what I dreaded has happened to me" (Job 3: 25).* We become subject to the things we fear. Fear attracts storms, ill winds and all sorts of demonic atrocities. Fear is one of the devil's gateways into our lives. On the other hand, faith in the Lord and His Word is the gateway to the blessings, joy and peace of the Lord. Fear welcomes the enemy while faith keeps him out! I believe that the disciples feared and dreaded the windstorm, even before their boat began to fill with water. The fear of the windstorm attracted the waters associated with the windstorm. Let the fear of windstorms of life depart, and let faith in God's Word fill your heart, that it might attract the corresponding blessings and promises of God.

After Jesus rebuked the wind and raging water; *the men became afraid, and marvelled, saying to one another, "Who can this be? For He commands even the winds and water, and they obey Him!"* After what Jesus did they still marvelled and questioned who He was. It is acceptable to marvel at the doings or works of the Lord, but let your marvelling be one of rejoicing in the awesome deeds of God's righteousness. Let ours be reverential fear of God and His mighty works. Jesus is who He says He is. The Word—Jesus does whatever He says He will do. *God is not a man, that He should lie, nor a son of man, that He should repent. Has He said, and will He not do? Or has He spoken, and will He not make it good? (Numbers 23:19 NKJV).*

As we daily travel with the Lord, we must realize that He is not oblivious to the windstorms that will come against us. It's paramount for us to remember, that Jesus is with us and in us—His vessels. He's already equipped us with His Word enabling us to rebuke the storms we'll face as we transition. Know and believe that daily we are armed with God's Word to face and overcome every trial and temptation. Never question the Word of God given and spoken to you to counteract the stormy winds. No matter how "little" it seems, the Word of God, like the crumbs, is able to do what God says it will do and will succeed in freeing you from the storms.

God is a faithful witness by reason of His Word—Jesus Christ, so don't question it, but rather speak it forth in faith; declare it and watch the peace of God rule in the affairs of your life! As you "cross over to the other side" never take your eyes of God's Word and promises. His Word is your instructor, the wind that leads you on, navigating the twists and turns on your journey.

As we've already seen, once Jesus allowed His disciples to get into a boat and go before Him to the other side, a storm blew up in the middle of the sea: *tossed by the waves, for the wind was contrary.* Jesus went to His disciples in the fourth watch of the night, walking on the sea. When they saw Him walking on the sea, they were troubled, saying, *"It is a ghost!" And they cried out in fear.* Jesus immediately spoke to them saying, *"Be of good cheer! It is I; do not be afraid" (See Matthew 14:22–33).*

Mark's interpretation of this encounter reveals something rather striking. He wrote, *He saw them straining at rowing, for the wind was against them. Now about the fourth watch of the night He came to them, walking on the sea, and would have passed them by (Mark 6:48 NKJV).* Mark's version says Jesus saw them struggling with the oars, and would have passed them by. In this scenario Jesus was not in the boat, but rather sent them on ahead. Once again, this journey was commanded by Jesus. Once again the sea and wind were raging against the disciples—those He sent on assignment. But once again, it came as no surprise to Jesus.

Jesus—the Word of God decided to walk toward them on the very thing (the sea) that was raging against His disciples. This is very significant. Once again, like the disciples and Joseph, you're caught in a "raging sea" accompanied by stormy winds. However, be encouraged that the "sea and winds" against you have attracted the attention of Jesus, and His Word is not far from rescuing you once again. The Lord always knows when to show up, and He will always present Himself in His own unique way—to deliver you out of "troubled waters."

Many are the afflictions of the righteous, but the Lord delivers him out of them all (Psalms 34:19). You might be caught in the middle of a "raging" situation time after time—where going back might seem just as dangerous and life-threatening as going forward. Be encouraged that Jesus is the Master over everything. He went to the men walking on the sea. You can only walk on that which you have mastery over. Be of good cheer; do not be afraid because the Word of God supersedes every storm you'll ever face. You might be in the middle of the storm, but Jesus has your back.

God, and not the devil, has absolute charge over every trial you encounter. This doesn't mean you'll never again face trials, but remember that when they come, it's time to surrender it all to Jesus, who will then work it out for your good.

Why then would Jesus see us like His disciples straining and struggling at what we are doing and pass us by? The operative words are *straining at rowing.* The sea and the wind were working against them once more, however, instead of applying the Word of God and speaking to the sea, they were *straining at rowing.* Sometimes we blame God for not coming to our rescue or for "passing us by." This happens when we fail to invite Jesus or His Word into our challenges.

These men were fishermen who thought they knew the sea and must certainly have faced raging storms in the past. Due to their experience they probably thought they could handle things as they had always done. Only this time the interference was diabolical. The term *"straining at rowing"* indicates that they were trying to solve problems in their own strength. We often do this without acknowledging Him or seeking His guidance. Many times, we think we have experience, so we can handle this trial the way we always have. The Lord can't help us if we continue doing things our way, neglecting the fact that the storm has caught His attention and His help is right on site, coupled with the fact that we're ignorant to the reality that this present storm is nothing like those we've experienced before.

The Lord is indeed our refuge and strength, a very present help in troubled times, however, He can't help us if or when we're too busy helping ourselves. Many say God helps those who help themselves. Newsflash!

Nowhere is this found written in the canon of scripture; this is not scriptural and has no biblical foundation! Sadly, Christians are often guilty of believing it's true, but it's actually the exact opposite of what God wants, which is complete dependence on Him. The disciples were so busy helping themselves that the Helper who was right there in their midst, would have passed them by, unable to help at all!

Notice the time their Helper intervened and helped. This was when they saw Him, though they cried out in fear thinking it was a ghost. When they took their eyes off rowing and looked to Jesus, crying out in fear, He responded to their fear and came to their aid. Their cries were a form of prayer as we read earlier. Jesus spoke words of comfort to then and told them, *"It is I; do not be afraid"* *(Matthew 14:27, Mark 6:50)*.

In like manner, when you and I cry out to the Lord, the Word of God presents Himself alive and powerful to us. He brings us comfort and reassures us that He's got our "backs." It was like Jesus was saying, "I've got your back, guys, no need to fear." Jesus has our "backs" as long as we're crying out to Him in faith and prayer, surrendering and committing things into His hands. He's right there to shield and shelter us from the storms. He's the refuge and tower we run to for safety *(See Proverbs 18:10)*.

Even then, Peter still doubted that it was Jesus who was walking on the sea, and said, *"Lord, if it is You, command me to come to You on the water."* Peter appeared ready to walk on water—the problem that had risen up against him; at the command of Jesus—the Word of God. Jesus told Peter, "Come." Matthew went on to explain, *and when Peter had come down out of the boat, he walked on the water to go to Jesus. But when he saw [e]that the wind was boisterous, he was afraid; and beginning to sink he cried out, saying, "Lord, save me!"* *(Matthew 14:28-30 NKJV)*.

Note that Jesus never calmed the sea before commanding Peter to come to Him. The Lord won't always calm your raging waves before telling you to *"come"* walk on stormy seas. In other words, the storms will not necessarily stop, nonetheless, Jesus wants us to come to Him despite the storms, by reason of His Word. His Word tells us that we can do all things through Christ who strengthens us *(Philippians 4:13)*. Through Christ Jesus we can walk on life's "raging seas" just as Peter walked to Jesus in the tumult. God expects us to walk on "raging seas," exercising mastery over trials and temptations even though they continue to rage around us.

Jesus is there with you, so keep your eyes on Him while you're walking through the storms. The moment Peter took his eyes off Jesus he began to sink. The moment we take our eyes off the Lord and His Word, we'll begin to sink and be blown away by the boisterous *"windstorms"* of life. What's on your mind this very second? What's robbing you of joy and peace? What has caused you to abandon God or take your eyes off His Word? What has robbed you of the intimate time you once had with the Lord?

Jesus has beckoned us to walk along the path that leads to Him. Along that path, like Peter, the Lord has empowered us to walk on "waves" that are meant to cause us to sink. But if our gaze remains fixed on Jesus, He will make a way through. However, we begin to "sink" into a sea of depression, bitterness, hurt, offense, fear and prayerlessness when we give our attention to the things that make us worry.

The sea was already raging when Peter walked on water before he became distracted by the raging sea. The enemy will always bring distracting winds our way. He does this in an effort to intensify what we're already facing, all because the enemy realises that in keeping our focus on Jesus and His Word, we gain the upper hand over any tempest. The devil realises that faith is rising and fear is sinking, therefore, to keep us bound in fear in order for us to "sink" in the storms, he releases distracting challenges against us.

The enemy uses all sorts of distractions to keep our eyes and attention off the Lord and His Word, if but for a moment; as our thoughts become preoccupied with issues, instead of doing what Jesus has commanded us to do in the midst of our challenges. In that split second of distraction, we can miss what God was about to show us and do in our lives. For all you know God was about to deliver you out of that trial, or He was about to grant you the solution you so desire to address the matter at hand.

Let's not allow the enemy to distract us, by causing us to be preoccupied with anything other than God's will and counsel, even in the storm. Each time we're about to break through, the devil sends distracting winds against us to disqualify us from a divine opportunity. Interestingly enough, trouble is also a personality and has a personality! The devil doesn't only use situations and challenges against us, but he also uses people to trouble, frustrate and distract us. Let no one come to you as trouble to distract you from gaining an upper hand over your trials.

The writer of Hebrews encourages us to look unto Jesus, the author and finisher of our faith *(Hebrews 12:2a, NKJV)*. As longs as we fix our gaze on the Lord Jesus and His Word, He will be faithful to complete what He started in and for us, and we'll in turn faithfully complete our journey with Him. Whilst sinking Peter cried out, *"Lord, save me!"* At least he did not say, *"Master, Master, I am perishing!"* No! He asked the Lord to save Him; he called upon the Word of God and tapped into the salvation of God.

Peter knew that Jesus—the very Word of God Himself, was able to save him; hence, he gave no credit to the devil at that point in time. Remember Job advises us that when we're cast down, it's our responsibility to declare the Word of God positively in faith, and God will save us. Even if you feel that you're going down for the third time, the salvation of the Lord, who is your present help in time of trouble—is nearer than you think. All you need to do is to ask the Lord to save you, just as Peter did. Those few words will grant you audience before the Lord.

Peter called out to Jesus to save him, *and immediately Jesus stretched out His* hand and caught him, and said to him, "O you of little faith, why did you doubt?" *And when they got into the boat, the wind ceased. Then those who were in the boat came and worshiped Him, saying, "Truly You are the Son of God" (Matthew 14:31–33 NKJV)*. It's evident that Peter was actually getting the lesson at hand. On that occasion, Peter didn't cry out that he was perishing—instead he asked the Word of God to save him. It's also important to note that the other disciples were no longer afraid. This time they came worshipping Jesus, identifying Him as the Son of God!

The disciples didn't question who Jesus was, nor were they fearful, though they still lacked complete faith. These men were God's work in progress, and they were certainly making progress. Our trials and stormy winds aren't meant to destroy us, but to mature us in God and His Word. Through the storms, our faith will be tested and built up, and as a result we'll be better able to grab hold of God's Word in every situation, whether good or bad, as evidenced by the worship we ascribe to Him through it all.

Once we recognize and take hold of the Word of God and declare what He says, the arm of the Lord will be revealed to us and rescue us from trials. Realize that there is no ghost present in your trials. There is no spirit or apparition! Refuse to see the enemy in your trials! Choose to see only Jesus in all you go through, even when it's orchestrated by the devil! The devil is behind it, but give no glory to him! Don't even speak his name; speak only the name of Jesus that is above every other name! The name of Jesus will safely bring you out of every storm.

See Christ in His form as Saviour, Healer, Redeemer, Provider, Friend, and everything He says He is. See Jesus coming to your aid, so don't shout like the disciples, *"It's a ghost!"* or "It's the devil!" Refuse to say, "It's the devil doing all this to me." Refuse to see Satan—Look to Christ by reason of the Word of God. Focus on Jesus who is far greater and more powerful than the devil and the storms. Recognize Jesus and His Word. Call Him into your situation, by speaking His Word into your trials and praising Him through it all.

Look to Jesus to save you that you may rise above diabolical winds, evil decrees and the reasoning and predictions of men, orchestrated to distract and destroy you. Speak His Word to rebuke distracting diabolical winds and the "raging sea." Jesus is in your vessel; you are equipped with His Word to rise above all odds and to rise up out of every evil plan of the enemy. Shift your focus back to the Lord and command your exaltation by God's Word, giving no attention to the devil!

God created all things including principalities, powers, and Satan himself. Can Satan now out-do the God who created him? No! Never! Impossible! Satan might be the instigator and orchestrator of the storms. However, God is the One whom the Psalmist wrote about when he said,

The voice of the LORD is over the waters;
The God of glory thunders;
The LORD is over many waters.
The voice of the LORD is powerful;
The voice of the LORD is full of majesty. *(Psalms 29:3-4 NKJV)*

The devil's voice is not over many waters, nor is he over many waters. Only the Lord and His voice command the many waters, and when He speaks, waters must hear and obey, so that when God speaks, situations must heed His commands and stop their tumult, instantly calm. In the midst of the stormy winds, "raging waters", trials and temptations, listen for the voice of the Lord and issue His command with the power-of-attorney given to you by Christ Jesus. See the Lord over the waters walking on the turbulent, boisterous winds and "raging seas" coming against you, as you speak forth His commanding Word.

At that point, let your faith arise, and be stirred, confident that you serve a God for whom all things are *possible (Matthew 19:26).*

God is the Master of impossibilities. He creates the possible out of the impossible. There's no failure in God, hence, there is no need to doubt Him—only believe and keep your gaze fixed on Him. Let Jesus be the centre of it all and take no journey without Him, or wander away on route to your destination. Our destiny is deeply entwined with His leadership; we simply can't get there without Him.

If we think we have arrived and the Word of God is neither with us nor in us, we are in fact deceiving ourselves. We cannot fulfil God's divine purpose without His Word. Sail on, knowing that if God has commanded us to "cross over to the other side", our safety is guaranteed, when we walk in faith, obedient to His command. Jesus has saved you before and you need not be afraid, because He'll do it again and again. The storm will not kill you or overpower you, but as the song writer so beautifully put it, *"With Christ in the vessel we can smile at the storm."*

CHAPTER SEVEN

Stay in the Boat or Die

From the previous chapter we saw that even though the boat was tossed about, no one attempted to abandon ship or jump overboard. Had they jumped overboard into the waters that were stirred by the windstorm, there's a good possibility some would've drowned. On both occasions though their vessels were under attack and their lives were in danger, they stayed in the boat. *(Luke 8:22-25, Matthew 14:22-33)*

Many times, when stormy winds blow against our vessels, we quickly respond by giving up—giving up on people, the church and at times, even God Himself. One might think, "I'm going to die anyway, so what's the point?" We allow fire, hail, snow, clouds and stormy winds to determine our destiny, forgetting that irrespective of these seasons, God's Word will still prosper in our lives. At times the boat that seems to be capsizing, actually turns out to be the boat of deliverance. One such occasion occurred when the Apostle Paul was "crossing over to the other side."

In Acts 27 we read that Paul ended up a prisoner in Rome. As they began that particular journey, they encountered dangerously contrary winds. Having sailed for many days, their journey was fraught with jeopardy. The Bible says:

Now when much time had been spent, and sailing was now dangerous because the Fast was already over, Paul advised them, saying, "Men, I perceive that this voyage will end with disaster and much loss, not only of the cargo and ship, but also our lives" (Acts 27:9-10 NKJV)

At times on our journey, we experience "winds" contrary to the will of God. Having faced contrary days, seasons and moments, things soon became difficult. As if the difficult challenges and storms weren't enough, life's situations can become dangerous and life threatening. At that point in time, like Paul, we begin to perceive the loss we might face as the winds beat against our lives.

Acts 27:11 (NKJV) says, *Nevertheless the centurion was more persuaded by the helmsman and the owner of the ship than by the things spoken by Paul.* Sometimes when "contrary winds" rise against us, we need to stop for a moment and realize that those issues could have been avoided if only we had heeded the Word of God, the instructions of the Holy Spirit or of those God has sent our way to reveal His will.

Having rejected the Word and counsel of God as spoken by Paul, those on the journey faced danger: *when the south wind blew softly, supposing that they had obtained their* desire, putting out to sea, they sailed close by Crete. *But not long after, a tempestuous head wind arose, called Euroclydon (Verse 13-14, NKJV).* Just like the crew, we might refuse the counsel of the Lord, all because things might have appeared calm, like the *south wind that blew softly;* causing the men to put out to sea. But as the journey continues, we find that we're suddenly overtaken by the enemy's deceptive devices and schemes. *"Euroclydon"* suddenly raises its head and begins to take us on the ultimate path to destruction.

When we notice situations going sideways in our lives, it's an indication that we need to make haste in consulting God and His Word. Many times, the trials we face could have been prevented, if only we had acknowledged the Lord, allowing Him to direct our paths according to His Word to us in *Proverbs 3: 5-6*. When we fail to invite the Lord into our contrary situations, and continue to walk it out on our own, we'll soon discover how difficult that situation can get.

When we fail to commit those situations to the Lord, it will get even more difficult to escape, even though at this stage we might still desire to break free. Consider a situation or relationship that is already contrary to the will of God for your life. You decided to be led by feelings and emotions and disregard the Lord, though you discover that it's time to let it go. However, because you're in so deep, breaking away becomes increasingly difficult. It's like being in the middle of the sea—turning back toward land is risky but going ahead is even more risky. You're then forced to stay right where you are, in no-man's land.

This difficulty then becomes dangerous as it affects more and more lives that could be destroyed if you stay where you are. The danger is not just to you and the other party or parties involved, but to others such as your family members, children, friends or loved ones, who will inevitably become casualties of something that started as a questionable situation—one that could have been prevented from the beginning. This dangerous relationship will result in lost families, lost friendships, lost hopes and dreams, lost peace and joy, lost faith and trust. Your children may be hurt or lost as the result of your decisions, even causing financial and marital struggles. Your destiny in God and the destinies of others are now at risk.

For a moment all might seem to have died down, only to find like *Euroclydon*, that tempestuous situations stare you in the face once again. Suddenly the challenge you thought had ended, sees it as an opportune time to attack you again with full force. Had you closed the gateway opened by that which was contrary, it would've shattered the power of the attack, shutting down the danger to your life and destiny.

By then, continuing the journey had become dangerous, as though the lesson was wasted. Making questionable choices, the disciples found a skiff from an island called Clauda, and secured it using cables to reinforce the ship's frame. And because *they were exceedingly tempest-tossed,* the next day they lightened the load on the ship (See verse 16-18). When faced with stormy winds, that's not the time to take on excessive weight, adding to the load.

What we need to do is resist, letting go of things God wants us to release. You're already being tossed by storms, so don't take excess weight on board, because it will only make things worse. When the storm is too much to bear, check the load you're carrying. Let God show you what you need to "throw overboard" in order to calm the raging storms—to help you to survive the journey.

The Lord doesn't want you to "jump overboard", but rather to lighten "your ship", and get rid of the excessive cargo that might attract even more storms. The excessive cargo might be someone you need to release. It might be a relationship, or even a spirit of unforgiveness. Remember you are still on the stormy sea and your "boat" is still *tempest-tossed.* In order to carry on, you'll need to travel light, to enable the boat to survive the storm and reach your destination unharmed.

God might not speak peace into the storm yet, but we need to remember that the journey ahead is still great. One need not carry excessive cargo and jeopardize the journey ahead, making life even more risky than it already is. Besides, when we travel light, it's easier to be led by the wind of God's Holy Spirit. It's easier for the Spirit of God to direct our vessels through the storm. We can be in the middle of tempestuous storms and perilous winds, but the wind of God's Holy Spirit is more than able to lead us safely through.

Even when we throw things "overboard" that are not in alignment with will of God, it doesn't mean that the trial or challenge is over. Paul informs us, *Now when neither sun nor stars appeared for many days, and no small tempest beat on us,* all hope that we would be saved was finally given up. *But after long abstinence from food, then Paul stood in the midst of them and said, (See verse 20, 21a NKJV).* We'll still experience days of gloom and darkness as our storms continue, tossing us in every direction. At times the nights may even seem longer than the days.

You might feel like giving up. However, after a *"long abstinence from food,"* after many days of fasting food or God's Word, after many days of God's silence, Paul stood up and spoke. It doesn't matter how dark the skies or how silent the Lord might appear, there will still be a release of the Word of God to encourage you in the midst of the storms. Paul stood up and said,

"Men, you should have listened to me, and not have sailed from Crete and incurred this disaster and loss. And now I urge you to take heart, for there will be no loss of life among you, but only of the ship. For there stood by me this night an angel of the God to whom I belong and whom I serve, saying, 'Do not be afraid, Paul; you must be brought before Caesar; and indeed God has granted you all those who sail with you.' Therefore, take heart, men, for I believe God that it will be just as it was told me" (verses 21-26 NKJV).

Paul gave the ship's occupants a word from God that their lives would not be lost; only the ship would be lost. It doesn't matter what storms we encounter; regardless of how perilous they seem, as long as we heed the voice of the Lord, we'll by no means suffer loss. It might seem as though you're losing now—it might seem like you're losing this battle. However, to God, your gain far supersedes what you think you've lost. You can never lose as long as you believe in God and His Word.

The Lord rather wants us to lose the "ship" or things that are carrying us that are not of Him. Many times we face turbulences in life as a result of the many vessels we find ourselves in and the many things that are piloting and steering our lives other than God's word and Spirit. I am sure the occupants of the ship were afraid to know the ship would be lost. They might imagine their lives flash before them, thinking, "How can we be saved if the ship is lost?" After all, the ship was carrying them and was their point of safety on a restless sea and facing a turbulent storm. To them, what Paul said might have made no sense.

This happens when our dependency and confidence is in that which is carrying us and not on God. We might think if we lose that which is the fuel behind our lives and survival, we will surely die. However, rest assured that if God allows what is carrying you other than His word to be destroyed, it is His way of letting you know you will not die but rather survive. What seems impossible with man is possible with God. To human beings, what God allows to be destroyed might seem like an eminent death sentence; to God, it is life and preservation.

There are places God is sending you; there are blessings yet to be received and divine assignments yet to be accomplished. The only way we will not survive the storms of life is when we do not heed to the voice of the Lord. As long as you are en route to where God wants you to go, no matter what comes our way, like Paul, as long as you rest in the Lord and His word, you will get there safely despite the storms.

On the fourteenth night of being tossed about at sea, about midnight, the sailors perceived they were approaching land. On measuring the depth of water, it was found to be 120 feet and shortly after that, 90 feet. Being afraid of being driven against rocks, they threw anchors from the stern of the ship and prayed for day to beak *(See Acts 27:27–29).*

No matter how long you have been tossed by the storms and struggles of life, and no matter how long the night and dark the season, know that you are approaching land. You might be in the midnight hour in your storm, wondering if the storm will come to an end and wondering if rescue and relief will come; rest assured you are approaching land—your time of deliverance.

At times you can see your deliverance; however, it does not mean that you will not come close to some "rocky" situations. In such time, look to the Lord to be your anchor as your deliverance and breakthrough approach. In order not to hit the enemy's rock, hold firm to Jesus Christ, our Rock. The songwriter wrote,

We have an anchor that keeps the soul
Steadfast and sure while the billows roll
Fasten to the Rock which cannot move
Grounded firm and deep in the Saviour's love
—Priscilla Jane Owens

In the storms of life, as the wind blows and as the water rages, let your faith be anchored, rooted, and grounded in the Rock, Jesus Christ, His word and promises. Fastened to Jesus, our Rock, it is certain that you will not be driven into or clashed with any diabolical rocks, rocky situations, or driven aground.

Weeping may endure for a night; and you may weep through the night and your midnight hour; however, daybreak will come with joy—joy will come in the morning *(See Psalms 30:5b)*. Whilst still caught in the strong winds and raging sea, adapt a posture of prayer like the sailors; pray for daybreak, pray for daylight, and rest assured in God that your morning is coming. Your joy and days of laughter are approaching.

It came to a point in time when the sailors were seeking to escape the ship. Paul warned the centurion and the soldiers, saying, *"Unless these men stay in the ship, you cannot be saved."* Not because you see land or catch a glimpse of rescue and relief; this does not mean you should, as it were, "jump ship." The stormy season you are facing is a process that should not be prematurely intercepted by you or anyone else. Trying to get out of the storm prematurely could end in death.

We are reminded in the word of God that there is a way that seems right to a man; however, its end is death. That path will soon be realised as a road to destruction *(See Proverbs 14:12, Proverbs 16:25)*. Attempting to "jump ship" could end in falling on diabolic rocks and falling into rocky situations, which may result in more harm and danger than the storm you are facing. To prevent the men from jumping overboard and remaining on the ship, *the soldiers had to cut away the ropes of the skiff and let it fall off.* For your safety and preservation, the Lord might allow some things to be cut off your life and taken away from you in order for you to remain "on board" and in the process.

After some time, Paul implored the men to take food and take nourishment whilst reassuring them once again of their preservation and safety. Having broken bread and giving thanks to God, they all ate. *So when they had eaten enough, they lightened the ship and threw out the wheat into the sea (See Acts 27:33–38).* When in the storms, be encouraged to nourish and feed your spirit-man with the word of God. Mediate on God's word day and night that you might prosper and succeed amidst adversity! The word of God will inevitably lighten your "ship" or vessel. God's word will break yokes and lift the heavy burdens, which are meant to cause you to "sink" into the raging seas of life and consumed by stormy winds. As the word of God lightens your spirit, you will be able to throw the excess weight "overboard" and out of your life, bringing you great calm and peace as you await daylight.

Finally, it came to pass when it was day; however, *they did not recognise the land.* God will do just as He said. He will take you out of the storms and stormy winds and bring you ashore. It is, however, paramount for you to recognise the "land", place, destiny, or blessings the Lord has placed before you and taken you into. The "land", place and destination, must look exactly like the "land" or blessings the Lord Himself has promised you. It must mirror the written and spoken word of the Lord for your life.

Whilst approaching land and letting go the anchor into the seas, hoisting the sail and heading toward shore, they struck a crosscurrent and ran the ship aground, causing the stern of the ship to *break up under the violent forces of the waves.*

Those who could swim made their way to shore, and the rest made their way *on heavy boards or pieces of the vessel.* And so it was that all escaped safely to land *(See Acts 27:39–44).*

Envisioning your breakthrough, still take care to submit to the leading of the Holy Spirit to ensure smooth entrance into your season and breakthrough. Be careful along the way to prevent unnecessary obstacles, stumbling blocks and "violent waves" that will try to hinder you getting "ashore." Paul and all the occupants of the ship made it safely to land—their destination. Having been through it all, *Acts 28* lets us know that Paul made it safely to Rome.

You will get through this storm, you will go through safely, and you will get to that designated place in God and lay hold of every word and promise He has for your life. The prophet Isaiah reminds us,

> *But now, thus says the Lord, who created you, O Jacob, and He who formed you, O Israel; "Fear not, for I have redeemed you; I have called you by your name; You are Mine. When you pass through the waters, I will be with you; and through the rivers, they shall not overflow you. When you walk through the fire, you shall not be burned, nor shall the flames scorch you. For I am the Lord your God, the Holy One of Israel, your Saviour . . . (Isaiah 43:1–3a NKJV).*

CHAPTER 8

Heading for Tarshish

Our lives will attract "stormy winds" if we allow the carnal things of the world to supersede the will of God, which clearly indicates that we're not running the race the Lord has set before us. *Hebrews 12:1(NKJV)* reads, *therefore, we also, since we are surrounded by so great a cloud of witnesses, let us lay aside every weight, and the sin which so easily ensnares us, and let us run with endurance the race that is set before us.*

Here, God's Word is reminding us that, many have suffered for the sake of the gospel; however, regardless of their suffering, they remained steadfast in faith, honouring the Lord in all they did, until death. Even today, Christians are expected to remain faithful to God, irrespective of the trials they encounter. This requires setting aside every sin that will prevent us from remaining faithful to the Lord—and persevering in times of storms.

The swiftness at which we start a race in the natural, does not determine how we will finish the race, or even whether we'll finish well. What matters is perseverance. As long as we persevere, we'll finish the race. It doesn't matter if others are growing faster than you are. You may think that the pace at which you're growing, is very slow, but what matters is that you finish the race that God has set before you, and remain steadfast against all odds, in all you do and say.

If the Lord has set a race before us, it's obvious that He's given us a divine mandate to fulfil. When sin, rebellion and insubordination dwell amongst us, we are running, but not the race that God has called us to run. Instead, we're heading for *"Tarshish"* and running away from the will and purpose of the Lord. The Bible brings to our awareness, the calamities encountered by the prophet Jonah, when he ran from the divine mandate that God had instructed him to fulfil.

The Bible says, *Now the word of the Lord came to Jonah the son of Amittai, saying, "Arise, go to Nineveh, that great city, and cry out against it; for their wickedness has come up before Me." But Jonah arose to flee to Tarshish from the presence of the Lord. He went down to Joppa, and found a ship going to Tarshish; so he paid the fare, and went down into it, to go with them to Tarshish from the presence of the Lord (Jonah 1:1-3NKJV).* Jonah had an instruction from the Lord, which was meant to cause the people of Nineveh to turn from their wicked ways and seek the face of God. But for whatever reason, Jonah chose not to go to the city, and headed elsewhere. He took matters into his own hands and ran away from the presence of the Lord. To aid him with his mission, a ship was waiting to take him from both the presence and will of the Lord.

As in the days of Jonah, the Lord has mandated Christians today to reach out to a wretched world, and preach the gospel, that many might repent of their sin and turn their hearts to the Lord. Like Jonah, some Christians have taken it upon themselves to do the opposite of what the Lord asked and do their own thing. Be aware that, when you decide to run away from the will of God, there will be a vessel ready and waiting for you. The enemy has vessels at the "ports" of our lives that are ready to take us to *"Tarshish"*–away from the will and purpose of God for our lives.

What vessels am I talking about? These are vessels of deception, sickness and disease, death (physical and spiritual), sexual immorality, poverty, marital conflicts, hatred, jealousy, and many other devices of the flesh. You name the vessels. The enemy has them all lined up at the "port" of your life. It is no wonder then, that our lives are filled with sorrow, oppression and "stormy winds." Could it be that some of us are not living in accordance to the will of the Lord? Could it be that the situation you now face is as a result of your choice to run from the presence, will and assignment of God?

When Jonah got to the ship, *he paid the fare*, and went down into it. When you and I try to run away from the will of the Lord, or reject the instructions of God, we will pay a price. That price might be sickness, barrenness, hardship, spiritual stagnation, contention, or the destruction of relationships and diverse trials. The devil will not allow you to be full of joy and happiness, once you turn your back on the Lord. The "vessels" of sin will take you where you want to go but will cost you far more than you want to pay.

You'll certainly have no rest in that place. Not only will you have the devil "breathing down your neck", but the Lord won't allow you to abort His will for His people and your life. Jonah ran away with a pseudo-assurance, that all was well. *But the Lord sent out a great wind on the sea, and there was a mighty tempest on the sea, so the ship he boarded was about to be broken up (Jonah 1:4).* The men aboard the ship were horrified, but Jonah decided to take a nap in the lowest parts of the ship.

At times, certain areas of our lives sometimes seem *"broken up"* and shattered. Marriages break up, threats come against our homes and families, ministries and relationships come under attack, and many experience broken hearts and dreams. Could it be the result of giving up on that which the Lord called us to do? A strong wind has shifted our lives out of alignment, and, much like Jonah, we can become overly relaxed and complacent about it.

To lighten the ship, the fearful sailors threw the cargo overboard, not knowing that Jonah was the one that needed to be thrown overboard. When you turn your back and "run away from the Lord" you also put the lives of others in danger. Running away from the will of God puts everyone you know in danger.

There are people who are dying in sin, while others need to be delivered, protected and guided in the things of God—and God has appointed you to become their deliverer and the instrument of His salvation. But what are you doing? Are you taking a rest from your divine assignment? The moment those who turn their backs on God enter the lives of other people, or try to attach themselves to others, those innocent souls suddenly begin to experience strong "turbulence" in their lives. What they need to do is to throw some of us *"overboard."* Or, maybe you need to throw some people and some things in your life *"over board."*

Either way, let's stop putting the lives of people in danger, because of our disobedience. The captain of the ship went to Jonah and asked him why he was resting, while they were about to perish. He pleaded with Jonah to call upon his God, that peradventure, He might have mercy on them and spare their lives. They then cast lots to ascertain who was responsible for the trouble that had befallen them. Of course, the culprit was identified as none other than the run-away—Jonah. After questioning him, the men realized that Jonah was a servant of the Most-High God—the God of the

Hebrews, whose power was known of by all. Jonah's God was the One, at whose name men trembled with fear *(Jonah 1:5-9)*.

Jonah introduced his God as the God of heaven, who made the sea and the dry land. Imagine the sailors saying, "Jonah, did you say the God who made the sea? Then you must be the one who has sent this mighty tempest upon us!" It wasn't long before the men discovered that Jonah was running from the Lord. They then said to Jonah, *"What shall we do to you may be calm for us?" –for the sea was growing more tempestuous.* He then instructed the men to, *"Pick me up and throw me into the sea; then the sea will be calm for you. For I know that this great tempest is because of me."* It was done as Jonah commanded, and the sea became calm *(Jonah 1:10-16 NKJV)*.

It goes without saying that you and I can become responsible for the stormy winds and the *"tempestuous seas"* that others are experiencing. When we fail to do what the Lord has assigned to us, our homes, children, the church or whatever God has assigned us over—comes under attack. When our children are getting off track, we need to ask ourselves when we last prayed for them. When the nations are at war, we need to ask ourselves if the church has truly been a house of prayer for the nations. Families, homes are being torn apart, but when was the last time you prayed for peace in your home? The sad thing is we're not exempted from the storms that come against those for whom we're assigned to either pray or preach to.

A lot of us, if not all, need to, as it were *"cast lots."* By no means do I suggest believers should gamble, or get involved in divination, but instead, *"cast lots"* in prayer. Ask the Lord, who or what is responsible for the *"turbulence"* and stormy winds you now face. Don't be surprised if the "lots" you cast, fall on you. Yes, usually we are the problem. I tell myself that if someone offends me, and I react contrary to the will of God, I become my own problem. By that I mean that if I live by the Word of God and His Word abides in me, I must be able to exercise self-control, and not deny God by my actions. The God in me must take pre-eminence at all times, over all the challenges I encounter. I choose to allow God to work on me. What about you?

God is the commander of heaven and the earth. All creation testifies of the glory and wonders of the Almighty. If you run away from the will and purpose of the Lord, He'll orchestrate situations and events that will identify you as a run-away. He may send a prophet to convict you of your sin, or He may choose to create other avenues such as this book, to let you know that you can't hide from His presence. You may hear a word in your Sunday morning service—one that speaks directly to your heart. Either way, repent and ask the Lord's forgiveness—that He might re-order your steps to His will. Take heed lest you become "swallowed" by your sin, iniquity, trials and temptations.

Jonah was swallowed by a giant fish, which the Lord had prepared to wait by the ship. It was in the belly of the whale where Jonah repented before God, for turning his back on Him. When Jonah was in a state of despair, he cried to the Lord, and the Lord had mercy on His servant. Jonah then said to the Lord, *"But I will sacrifice to You with the voice of thanksgiving; I will pay what I have vowed. Salvation is of the Lord" (Jonah 2:1-8, 9).* What has entrapped you or constrained you? Like Jonah, you might need to honour a vow you made to the Lord in order to break loose from that bondage. Sometimes addictions can be bondage, however, keeping a vow can break that addiction. If you vow not to go back to what God has taken you out of, then keeping that vow will lead to your deliverance.

According to the Scripture, the man of God renewed his vow unto the Lord, and the fish vomited him onto dry land. Jonah was caught in a situation, where he had nowhere to run and no one to run to—except God. He had to run back to the one he was running from. Jonah realized the hard way that, in all things, the Lord has the final word. After that, he was given a second chance to preach to the city of Nineveh. The Bible says, *Now the word of the Lord came to Jonah a second time, saying, "Arise, go to Nineveh, that great city, and preach to it the message that I tell you". So Jonah arose and went to Nineveh, according to the word of the Lord (Jonah 3:1-3a).*

When the Lord grants you a second chance, seize that opportunity to do what the Lord instructed you the first time. Arise and do! Act upon that which the Lord commanded you. When we're delivered out of the stormy winds, it's in order to be used to fulfil the purposes and will of the Lord. It's not for us to relax and again become complacent. So, we'd better be intentional and be about our Father's business. One needs to be focused on what the Lord has commanded and be intentional about carrying out His instructions.

Some of us need to renew our vows with the Lord. We need to go back to the Lord and tell Him, that we're willing to go wherever He sends us, and we're willing to do what He tells us. He's abundant in mercy, full of grace and compassion. Remember, the enemy is waiting with a vessel to carry you along the path of destruction. However, God is also waiting with a vessel to arrest you and bring you to your knees. Are you going to take the easy way out, by willingly returning to the Lord? Or, do you prefer the hard way? You choose.

It's a sin to make a vow to the Lord and not honour it. Once you become born again, you've made a vow to the Lord. We even promised the Lord to go where He sends us. Many times, we vowed not to do the things God disapproves of, yet we end up doing them anyway. Or we promise to do what the Lord asked of us, and we don't comply. At the appointed time when we are called by the Lord to do His will, we're either too busy or not ready. Christians want to dictate to the Lord, by telling Him what they can and cannot do. We do it, not only in words but by our actions. We only make matters worse for ourselves when we reject the Lord. It's time for us to speak the word of our Lord Jesus to the Father, which says, *"Nevertheless, not as I will, but as you will" (Matthew 26:39 NKJV).* These words not only carry your deliverance from the storms and turbulence of life, but set you back on course in order to fulfil your divine mandate. Disobedience will attract stormy winds. We need to surrender totally to God and His will for our lives.

In the end, the servant of the Lord—Jonah, took his mandate seriously, and went to the city of Nineveh to declare to them, that which the Lord had told him. The city repented and God had mercy on the people. And God relented from the disaster that He had said He would bring upon them, and He did not do it *(Jonah 3:1-9, 10).* After Jonah had carried out his divine mandate, he became angry with the Lord. Jonah told the Lord, *"Ah Lord, was not this what I said when I was still in my country? Therefore, I fled previously to Tarshish; for I know that You are a gracious and merciful God, slow to anger and abundant in lovingkindness, One who relents from doing harm. Therefore now, O Lord, please take my life from me, for it is better for me to die than to live!" (Jonah 4:1-3).*

Finally, we realize why Jonah fled to *Tarshish.* He didn't want the Lord to show mercy to those who had sinned against Him. Jonah was angry with God for withdrawing His anger from the city of Nineveh. Who are we to tell the Lord who to forgive and who not to forgive? Like Jonah, the Lord has instructed some of us to warn others of their sin, that they might repent and receive His forgiveness. But instead of warning them, we choose not to instruct them according to all the Lord has said to us. Why? Is it because we don't like them? Is it because of what we have heard others speak about them? Or, are we offended, because like Joseph, they're responsible for the trials we suffer?

Who are we to withhold the Word of the Lord from others, thus choosing to put their eternity in jeopardy? What if someone had chosen to run away from the will of God when He asked them to witness to us? Would we not still be dying in our sin? Would you and I have had the freedom that we now have in Christ Jesus if they hadn't obeyed? It doesn't matter what they've done to us, the Lord has called us to minister to those dying in sin. As believers, the indifference we display toward each other, is, in itself, a sin.

We expect the Lord to tell us what's required of us in order to live a life pleasing to God. So why is it that some Christians refuse to minister to others as the Lord requires? If you have ever withheld a word from a brother or a sister, or from anyone—now is your opportunity to repent before the Lord. If we decide to disobey the Lord, then let's stop asking Him for His anointing, because those kinds of things disqualify us. The anointing of God is not for ourselves, but is for the sole purpose of fulfilling the will of God. Don't seek His gifts, if you have no intention of using them to do His will. Don't seek the Lord if you have no intention of obeying His Word. Jesus is not merely a trophy that we seek, that we leave on a shelf once we acquire Him.

Don't be angry when you witness the glory of God in the lives of those you consider unworthy. For all you know, they're in unity with God and His will. Rejoice when the "lost sheep" return to the fold of God, and welcome them with open arms. Jonah's anger is evidence that he was still running away from the will of God. When the Lord instructs us to perform His will, we need to exercise obedience in both words and deeds. The Lord desires truth in the inward and outward parts of our being. There's no point in carrying out the will of God, yet rebel in our hearts. It's like telling someone that you love him when you really don't. Our will, emotions, and intellect, need to be in line with the will of the Lord.

We as Christians need to die completely to self, in order for the will of God to unfold, and be made manifest in their lives. Remember what happened to Queen Vashti when King Ahasuerus summoned her to attend the royal feast? The Book of Esther tells us that she refused to attend the royal feast as commanded by the king. The king became angry and sought the counsel of his wise men regarding the action that should be taken against the queen, for the wrong she committed against him *(Esther1:1-15)*.

One of the king's men called Memucan, answered the king saying, *"Queen Vashti has not only wronged the king, but also the princes, and all the people who are in all the provinces of King Ahasuerus. For the queen's behaviour will become known to all women, so that they will despise their husbands in their eyes, when they report, 'King Ahasuerus commanded Queen Vashti to be brought in before him, but she did not come'. This very day the noble ladies of Persia and Media will say to all the king's officials that they have heard of the behaviour of the queen. Thus there will be excessive contempt and wrath"* (Esther 1:16-18NKJV).

Memucan went on to say, *"If it pleases the king, let a royal decree go out from him, and let it be recorded in the laws of the Persians and Medes, so that it will not be altered, that Vashti shall come no more before King Ahasuerus; and let the king give her royal position to another who is better than she. When the king's decree which he will make is proclaimed throughout all his empire (for it is great), all wives will honour their husbands, both great and small"* (Esther 1:19-22).

All that Memucan suggested pleased the king, and Vashti was dethroned as queen. This is what has happened to many believers who refused the Lord's command to appear before Him. All the king wanted was to show off the beauty of his queen. When the Lord summons us to do His will, He too desires to not only show off His beauty, but also the beauty of God in us. He desires to use us to display His power, love, and mercy. Running away from

Him or refusing to heed to His voice, causes us to be dethroned from our position of authority, making us vulnerable to the enemy's ploys. The "vessel" of rebellion will always carry us to a place where great danger exists. Once you are out of God's will, you're heading for destruction and sailing on "stormy seas," because you have deliberately walked out from under His protective covering.

The one that was appointed as queen in Vashti's stead was a young woman, called Esther. Esther was taken against her will, to join the many young virgins, from whom the king would choose his future bride and queen. Though Esther was taken against her will and placed in the king's palace, she never rebelled by trying to escape from his presence. Instead, she humbled herself, and did what was required of her—to prepare for the mandate that the Lord had given her. *(Esther 2:1-7)*

The humility displayed by the Lord's handmaiden enabled her to find favour in the sight of the eunuch custodian, Hegai. Immediately, Esther was removed to the best place in the house of the women, and she was given beauty products to help in her preparation for one night with the king. Hegai instructed Esther in all her ways, and though she knew she could be the next queen of Persia, she never thought herself as being too "proud" to take sound advice from a common eunuch. *(Esther 2:8-11)*

The preparation for all the candidates would take one year, according to their custom. At the end of their preparation, all the ladies would be invited into the king's presence. Each candidate was given that which she desired to take from the women's' quarters to the king's palace. Then the ladies each went in to the king, and after they returned, they would never enter the king's presence again, unless he sent for them. When it was Esther's turn the word of the Lord reads, *she requested nothing but what Hegai the king's eunuch, the custodian of the women, advised.* Esther found grace and favour in the sight of the king, and was crowned queen instead of Vashti. *(Esther 2: 12-18)*

It would appear as though the other candidates had their own agendas for being queen of Persia. Their focus was somewhat different from Esther's, in that, they appeared to be interested in themselves, whereas Esther's concern was in pleasing the king. She wanted to know the will of the king, in order to make her will his own, and that's why she heeded to the voice of the one who knew the king better than all others, Hegai the eunuch.

Following her appointment as queen, the Lord then decided that Esther was ready for the divine mandate for which she'd been prepared. It came to a time when Haman (a hater of the Jews), was promoted by the king, above all the princes who were with the king. Everyone bowed before Haman, except Mordecai, the uncle of Esther, who would bow to no one except Almighty God. As a result, Haman became angry and decided to kill all the Jews throughout the kingdom, for the sake of Mordecai, who was also a Jew. *(Esther 3:1-7)*

Haman went to the king and said, *"There is a certain people scattered and dispersed among the people in all the provinces of your kingdom; their laws are different from other people's, and they do not keep the king's laws. Therefore it is not fitting for the king to let them remain. If it pleases the king, let a decree be written that they be destroyed, and I will pay ten thousand talents of silver into the hands of those who do the work, to bring it into the king's treasuries"* (Esther 3:8-9).

The king consented to Haman's plot, and a decree was written and proclaimed throughout the King's provinces, to kill all the Jews. To summarise the story, the matter got back to Mordecai, who in turn sent a message to the queen informing her of Haman's plot to annihilate the Jewish population. Esther was afraid to petition the king, as he had not sent for her, for thirty days. This she related to Mordecai, that whosoever entered the presence of the king without being summoned, would face death, unless the king held out the golden scepter to him, that he might live. Mordecai's reply to the queen was that if she refused, she would not escape death, and if she remained silent the Lord would raise up another to deliver His people. (Esther 3:10-15, Esther 4:1-14)

The queen took it upon herself to proclaim a fast throughout the Jewish population. She also instructed her maidservants to fast. The queen said, *"And so I will go to the king, which is against the law; and if I perish, I perish!" (Esther 4:15-17).* To conclude the matter, Esther went before the king, and found favour in his sight. In the end, the Jews were saved and Haman was hanged on the gallows he prepared for Mordecai.

The point of this illustration is that Esther was prepared by the Lord for the task He had appointed her to do. The preparation did not come easily, yet, she chose to endure rather than running back to the life she knew. Some of us, instead of allowing the Lord to prepare us for our divine assignment, will turn our backs on Him and return to the life we once knew. We tell the Lord that it's too hard to be His servant—that we would rather board the vessels of the devil, than conforming to the will of God.

At first, Esther was afraid to enter the courts of the king without being summoned, however, Mordecai reminded her that, if she ran away from the will of the Lord, He would appoint someone else to fulfil the mandate she abandoned. Esther was willing to die for the sake of saving her people; she was willing to die in order to fulfil the will of God. Instead of running away, she faced the situation head on, putting her trust in God.

Esther could have lost her life, but the Lord tells us to come boldly to the throne of grace, that we may obtain mercy and find grace to help in time of need *(Hebrews 4:16)*. But how many of us run to the Lord when we're faced with a difficult situation? Do you find it easy to run to God, or is it easier to run away? Are you willing to die to your will, that the will of God might be made manifest? Are you willing to die to the flesh, in order to save others?

If you run away from the will of the Lord, you will definitely perish along your journey. When you turn your back on the Lord, He will send someone else to do His work. But as for you, your end will be that of death, and not just spiritually; you will notice that suddenly everything around you begins to die. Your marriage, health or finances might begin to deteriorate, so that your life is suddenly overtaken by ever-increasing "turbulence."

What have you done with gifts the Lord has given to you? Have you buried them? Or are you using your talents wisely to increase the kingdom of God? When Esther chose to honour the Lord, she became the queen and co-ruler of 127 provinces. When we're faithful in the little the Lord has given us, He'll make us rulers over much. We'll experience peace, quietness and rest when we heed the will of God. However, if we're unfaithful with what the Lord has called us to do, He will take that which He has given to us, and give it to another. *(Luke 19:11-27, Matthew 25:14-30)*

We can't expect God to shower us with His blessings, when we're disobedient to His will. The Lord says, *"Give and it will be given to you: good measure, pressed down, shaken together, and running over will be put into your bosom. For with the same measure that you use, it will be measured back to you" (Luke 6:38).* If you don't give of your service to the Lord, how then do you expect to receive the abundance of His blessings? Each time God commissions you to perform a task, there's a blessing waiting for you on the journey. You can't reap where you haven't sown. You can't run away from the will of the Lord, and expect to be blessed. The blessings of God are not found on route to rebellion and disobedience.

The more you use your gifts and talents to obey the directions of the Lord, the more you'll receive from Him. Running away profits you nothing, except "turbulence." Just remember that, when you cause the kingdom of God to suffer loss, due to your disobedience, you also cause the enemy to make progress. Who is your master, the Lord or the devil? Who are you serving? Choose this day, for to serve the Lord is to profit, and to submit to the devil is to suffer loss and inherit persecution, hardship, temptation and stormy winds.

What vessel are you travelling in? Are you on a ship heading for *Tarshish?* Or, are you in the vessel of the Holy Spirit, heading into the will of God? Let go and let God do a marvellous work in your life. Let the beauty of the King's love be demonstrated to others, who are perishing and dying in sin and darkness. Be the candle of God that brings light to the darkness of this world. It's never too late to go before your King. You have nothing to fear. His scepter of love is already extended to you. Just touch it in submission to His will, demonstrating that you're willing to enter His presence, willing to do His will. In that place, He's willing to give all you need to fulfil His will.

You do not serve a wicked and cruel Lord, but rather, a God of love, mercy and compassion. He's always willing to take your hand and lead you back to Him, if only you let Him. Purpose in your heart today, to pay the vow you've made before the Lord. Let's turn from our wicked ways, that we might be healed of the afflictions brought upon us through rebellion and disobedience.

God is not interested in our carnal pursuits, but rather that which is important to Him—saving the souls of those dying in sin. His priority is to rescue the captives from the hands of Satan and returning them to the place by Him on the "Rock." Let's take the "staff" of the Lord in our hands once again, and begin to gather the flock into His sheep fold. In the words of our fore-runner, *"If we perish, we perish."* Begin to glean from the harvest that God has set before you. Be a faithful labourer in all you do. May your reward be great, as you diligently seek to do the will of God. And may He deliver you from the "turbulence" you encounter.

CHAPTER 9

Stand Still and See

The Word of the Lord reads,

Now the LORD *spoke to Moses, saying: "Speak to the children of Israel, that they turn and camp before Pi Hahiroth, between Migdol and the sea, opposite Baal Zephon; you shall camp before it by the sea. For Pharaoh will say of the children of Israel, 'They are* bewildered by the land; the wilderness has closed them in.' Then I will harden Pharaoh's heart, so that he will pursue them; and I will gain honor over Pharaoh and over all his army, that the Egyptians may know that I *am* the LORD." *And they did so.*

Now it was told the king of Egypt that the people had fled, and the heart of Pharaoh and his servants was turned against the people; and they said, "Why have we done this, that we have let Israel go from serving us?" So he [a] *made ready his chariot and took his people with him. Also, he took six hundred choice chariots, and all the chariots of Egypt with captains over every one of them. And the* LORD hardened the heart of Pharaoh king of Egypt, and he pursued the *children of Israel; and the children of Israel went out with boldness. So the Egyptians pursued them, all the horses and* chariots of Pharaoh, his horsemen and his army, and overtook them camping by the sea beside Pi Hahiroth, before Baal Zephon.

And when Pharaoh drew near, the children of Israel lifted their eyes, and behold, the Egyptians marched after them. So they were very afraid, and the children of Israel cried out to the LORD. Then they said to Moses, "Because there were no graves in Egypt, have you taken us away to die in the wilderness? Why have you so dealt with us, to bring us up out of Egypt? *Is* this not the word that we told you in Egypt, saying, 'Let us alone that we may serve *the Egyptians'? For it would have been* better for us to serve the Egyptians than that we should die in the wilderness."

And Moses said to the people, "Do not be afraid. Stand still, and see the salvation[b] of the LORD, which He will accomplish for you today. For the Egyptians whom you see today, you shall see again no more forever. The LORD will fight for you, and you shall hold[c] *your peace" (Exodus 14:1-14 NKJV).*

Here we have a scenario in the Word of God, where the children of Israel were in bondage for many years. They came under hard labour, struggles and various kinds of hardship, however, there came a time when God delivered them. Just before they left, the children of Israel plundered the Egyptians of their goods, after which God led them out of Egypt via the wilderness. As if it was not enough for the people of God to pass through the wilderness, whilst on their journey, God gave the children of Israel a command to encamp between Migdol and the sea which was opposite Baal Zephon.

Migdol, or Migdal, is a Hebrew word which means a high place as in a tower, an elevated stage or a raised bed (within a river) or a strongly fortified place. Baal Zephon which is opposite from where God commanded His people to encamp—its name was given to a storm god. This was the journey of the children of Israel as they came out of bondage, only to find themselves in a wilderness, and if that wasn't enough, they found themselves between a high place and the sea. To add insult to injury, they were caught in "storms" of life that were blowing at high speed.

Life's challenges can sometimes drive us into a wilderness when there is a lack in our lives—something that needs to be fulfilled. You're in the wilderness with a tower behind you and the sea before you. On top of that, the storms of life are raging around you. Where will you go? What will you do? You're caught in an extremely difficult situation—between a rock and a hard place. There are enemies before and behind you, enemies behind you and impossibilities ahead of you—danger before and danger behind you. You can't retreat, neither can you go forward. You're shut up on the right and the left. What do you do and where do you go?

And the storms of life are blowing, symbolic of the trials and situations we encounter on a daily basis, though we are carriers and conduits of the blessings of God. However, when God told them, "Encamp at this place between Migdol and the sea", where there was no room for escape; the command of the Lord to the children of Israel was to "Stand still." When you find yourself in difficult situations, hardship and diverse trials, and the Lord tells you to "Stand still", will you be able to stand still?

When the Lord tells us to stand still, it will not always be at a place that is free from danger and problems. It is when we are in a place of extreme difficulty, where to us there is no hope of escape. But God will still say "Stand still. I have commanded this encampment; I have asked you to take a pause where you are. I have put as it were a "comma" and a "semi-colon" here at this point in the journey of your life."

God knows where we are, but when He tells us to stand still, are we able to stand still. Inherent in human beings is the ability to always have a plan B. We often always have to find a route of escape; and we always have to do something to try and fix the situation. In 1 Samuel chapter thirteen, the Philistines came against King Saul and the children of Israel in their chariots, multitudes and numbers. Samuel the prophet told Saul he was coming to him at a particular and set time. Saul was so fearful of the Philistine army, and though he had to do something to help his people and himself. He though he had to fix his situation and map his way out of the impending danger and defeat.

What the prophet Samuel was in fact saying to Saul was, "stand still am coming." However, out of fear Saul sacrifice to God; and right there and then the prophet Samuel showed up and said, *"You have done foolishly."* Because Saul could not stand still and wait of God, Samuel told him, *"Today the Lord has torn the kingdom from your hand"*, and God gave it to one who knew how to stand still. David fought many battles and encountered many trials, he had many enemies; and even had to hide in a cave. Even though David found himself hiding in a cave, he was still a leader and the grace of God was still upon his life. God torn the kingdom of God from the hands of Saul and gave it to David; a man who knew how to be still and wait upon the Lord, whilst in a seemingly difficult situation.

Will you be like King Saul who couldn't wait on God when his enemies came upon Israel in overwhelming numbers and, feeling he had to do something, he couldn't wait on the prophet Samuel, but committed an unlawful sacrifice? When you are praying for that miracle, praying for that blessing, you are praying for that breakthrough; yet you cannot see a way out of your challenging situation? However, the Lord still says to you, "Stand still."

Sometimes as Christians we know how to work our own miracles. We know how to try and tailor-make things. Many allow the enemy to ask, "Are you crazy? What are you doing standing still, doing nothing?" Many allow the enemy to tell them they need to do something; because that is the nature of human beings, always have to interfere, thinking God needs our help. We think we must do something to try fix a situation that has gone wrong or going wrong. Many always try to change or create and manipulate a situation hoping it will turn out for their good; creating their own miracles—but God says, "Stand still so you can see what, not you, but I God will do in your life!" It's not about us, or what we are going through; rather is all about what God will do and is about to do if we only learn to stand still at His command.

God says no matter how boisterous the wind and how dangerous the storms, "Stand still!" The devil will tell you to march forward and pray for a miracle, do something fast, try this, try that. Don't just stand there, try to fix things in your own strength. The devil might say, "Perform your own miracle, make it happen." But God continues to says, "Stand still, and see the salvation of the Lord, which He will accomplish for you today. Will you be able to just be quiet and stand still and do nothing?

How many times have we missed a season or divine moment all because we felt we had to do something like Uzzah, we had to put our hand out to help steady the ark of God or help God. The bible reads *"And when they came to Nachon's threshing floor, Uzzah put out his hand to the ark of God and took hold of it, for the oxen stumbled. Then the anger of the LORD was aroused against Uzzah, and God struck him there for his error; and he died there by the ark of God." (2 Samuel 6:6-7 NKJV)*

Sometimes we try to stay and steady the things that are unsteady and shaking in our lives. God doesn't need us to stabilise the things that are unstable in our lives. How many times do we interfere with what God is doing all because we can't wait? If we want our time of waiting to be shortened, and the solution to be simple, we need to stop helping God. Stop interfering in God's business! Stay out of God's business! But if we choose to stand still, wait patiently for the salvation of the Lord and on God's divine intervention, it will not be too long before we hear the Lord say, "Move forward" *"And the LORD said to Moses, "Why do you cry to Me? Tell the children of Israel to go forward."(Exodus 14:15 NKJV)*

When God says, "Stand still", it is because He knows our efforts have expired, our strength have expired, that which He has asked and commanded us to do have expired. Therefore, He does not need our help; all He wishes for us to do is, stand still. God wants us to rest and watch Him move and perform on our behalf. It is by no means easy to stand still; but we need to realise that, that which God desires to do in our lives, no one else, not even us, can do it for ourselves. What God is desirous of doing in our lives is impossible with man; but possible with Him.

God at time enters a bilateral covenant with us; whereby we need to come in agreement with Him and His word, to make something happen, or bring some things to pass in our lives. Then, there is the unilateral covenant, whereby God does not need us to perform; He goes solo on this one—God all by Himself, not requiring our input or agreement. Such unilateral covenant does not involve our effort, strength or faith—just God.

Why are you crying? Why are you fearful? Why are you murmuring? When we are not at a place of stillness there is no way we can see what the Lord is doing in the midst of our storms. Refusing to stand still, all one will see is the storm and not the God who is over the storm; nor the God present in the storm. If our eyes are not on God we cannot see and will not see; if our eyes are not fixed on God we cannot know. We will only begin to see and know what God is doing when we stand still in the midst of the storms.

In recalling Jeremiah chapter 32, Jeremiah was told by the Lord, that, he the king of Judah—Zedekiah and his people would be taken into captivity by the king of Babylon. Their homes, land, and possessions would be destroyed and burnt with fire. God told Jeremiah that King Zedekiah would be taken captive and though he fights with the Chaldeans, he would not succeed. When God tells us to wait and stand still; lets us not try to fight our way out of the storm in our own strength, as the only thing this guarantees is us losing the battle. We need to remain still until the word of God visits us or comes to us.

God told the children of Israel, *"Do not fear to go down to Egypt" (Genesis 46:3).* Do not be afraid to be caught in the storms of live, do not be afraid when caught in a seemingly difficult situation; because the Lord will visit you and bless you. God told Jeremiah King Zedekiah would be in captivity until the Lord visits him. He told His servant, however, in that land that God was about to destroy; Jeremiah was to buy a field. God gave him an instruction that he should take the title deed for the land he was to buy, sign it and put it in a jar of clay that it may last for many days or a long time.

It is a though Jeremiah said, "God really, I should buy a field here." The Lord responded, *"Behold, I am the LORD, the God of all flesh. Is there anything too hard for Me?" (Jeremiah 32:27 NKJV).* Jeremiah acted in obedience to all the Lord had said and bought the field, signed it in front of witnesses, and placed the title deed in a jar of clay. We might be in captivity, caught in a raging storm, appear to have been destroyed, with nowhere to go, but there's a title deed that God has placed in you and I, the jar of clay and that when we get to the Migdol and Red Sea experience; that word or title deed is meant to be hidden in our hearts. It is by reason of that word, God will bring us out.

When God says "Stand still", He is telling us to recall to mind His promises, recall to mind what He has done for us in the past and to remember His faithfulness towards us. He is expecting us to recall to mind the word He have to us, like Jeremiah, before we enter that storm. God always gives us a redemptive word; that redemptive word is given before we enter any storm or given situation. Before we became sick, God tells us in His word, by His stripes we **were** healed. Before we became sick or in need of any deliverance; Jesus was already our Saviour and Deliverer. He made provision for us before we lack or were in want or need.

God said, "I will supply your needs". He knows that before you and I enter that wilderness, He is the one who supplies and has supplied. Our needs were met in Christ Jesus before we became in need. Jesus said to Martha, *"I am the resurrection and the life"*, not I will be, but *"I am"*. The word of God is always given to us before we encamp in our storms and trials. This word is meant to bring us into a state of stillness in times of despair and uncertainty; and enable us to wait patiently for Him to get us out of that seemingly impossible situation.

Why do we cry in fear and unbelief? *"Behold, I am the LORD, the God of all flesh. Is there anything too hard for Me?"* says the Lord. What is the trial and storms you are facing? Is there anything too difficult for the Lord? What is that mountain, that Migdal or Migdol, that tower that is in front of you? What is that Baal Zephon blowing all around you? What sea or impossibility is in front of you? God is the God of all flesh, is there anything too difficult for Him to handle? Why then do we fear and murmur before the Lord?

When Abram separated from Lot, God told him to *"Lift your eyes now and look from the place where you are"*. We need to lift up our eyes from murmuring, the complaints, the unbelief, the fear, the situation you think is impossible to get out of. It is only when we lift up our eyes from looking at Migdol, Baal Zephon—the storms of life and the sea; that we can see what God is doing and about to do. As long as our eyes are focused on the negativity, the storms and challenges of life; we will never see God, because we are looking at the wrong place.

Lift up your eyes and see; there is a land ahead of you, there is a possession beyond the *Red Sea*, there is an inheritance beyond *Migdol*; and there is a peace and quietness beyond *Baal Zephon*. As long as we keep our eyes on these three things, how can we see? In the disciples *"crossing over to the other side"* as instructed by Jesus; Jesus knew Baal Zephon—the storm god was about to raise its head, He knew the trials were about to come, He knew the tribulation would come, He knew the storm would be blowing at its highest speed; but He knew He was and is God. He is the God above every storm, the God above every gods, He is the King above every king and the Authority above every other authority.

He knew He was in their boat; the Word was in their vessel or jar of clay. God arose, Jesus arose, and He who is the Wind and breath of God arose; and calm Baal Zephon with the command, *"Peace Be Still"*. Baal Zephon had to retreat at the command of its Creator and the One's who voice is upon many waters—Jesus Christ.

Stand still! The word of God tells us, *"Having done all, stand"* (See Ephesians 6:13). We need to know when we get to that place of having done all. Sometimes we have done all; and we are not aware we have done all. We have expired the *having done all,* and need to know when we have in fact done it all. Having done all, stand and put on the armour of God; put on the word God gave you to overcome the storm and stand still in the midst of the storm. Take shelter in the word of God. Stand having done all; we have expired *having done all*; just stand still and watch God. Don't fidget around like a child restless because of having done nothing and wanting to touch or do something. Stand, having faith in God because the battle we face is not ours; it is of the Lord. Be at peace, be quiet and find rest in God's holy word.

After some time, God called Jeremiah and His people out of Babylon's captivity. The God who made that land, barren, desolate and famished brought back His people from captivity to their land. He caused His people to *move forward* to repossess their land by reason of the title deed. He said, *"Why are they crying to me, why are you so fearful, tell the people of God to move forward."* God has given us His rod of authority—His word, and all we need to do is stretch it our over that challenge, speak to the storms using the **rod** of God's word. God has given you and me His sceptre of authority by which we part difficult situations in order *to cross over to the other side.*

Yesterday we were in Egypt but God called us out! Yesterday we were in bondage and sickness but God called us out! Yesterday we were impoverished, but God blessed us! We were broken, barren and impotent, we were without a voice and without hope; and our God rescued, saved, redeemed and justified us through Christ Jesus our Lord. And today by reason of His Word, God is calling us, you and I—the church, out of captivity and out of the storms once again!

There is a moving forward, there is a divine advancement. God is about to fast-forward your life! He is about to accelerate you! But He says "Stand still, that you might see and watch Me move and perform wonders on your behalf." Our God is a God of miracles, signs and wonders—God is the same yesterday, today and forever! What he did in our lives before; He can do it again all for His glory and for His name sake. God's name is at stake, so fear not! He will get you out! Only believe. He knows the storms of life are raging; He knows you're caught between Migdol and the Red Sea, but He says to move forward and cross over.

Move forward in faith! Move forward in your mind! Move forward in hope and confidence in Your God! Stretch the word of God over the stormy winds.

When God tells us to stand still, it does not mean that our journey has ended. In travelling home for example, we may take three buses to our destination. In getting to the bus we walk from say our place of work; and in getting to the first bus stop what do we do? We stand still and wait for the bus to come. We get on the first bus which takes us to another destination, still not home, we get off the bus and at the same stop; what do we do again? We stand still and wait for the second bus to arrive. Having gotten on second the bus, we get off the next designated stop and what do we do? Stand still and wait for the final bus to arrive; and when it does, we get on that bus which then takes us to our final destination.

In the kingdom of God, and our lives as believers, there are many stand still moments. However, the standing still does not mean you will not get to that designated place, it does not mean you and I will not fulfil divine purpose, it does not mean that the promise of God will not be made manifest. The only time we will miss a bus is when we are at the bus stop on our phones looking down, too busy doing our own thing; looking here, looking for help there, looking for plan B, C, D, E F, G. We finish the alphabet and start again; keep looking in every direction; and by the time we lift our heads, we say "Wow! The bus is gone!"

This is the only time one will miss a moment of the move of God. We will still get to our destination; the only thing is— it will take us a longer time and be delayed for no reason. A lot of time we do not come into the perfect will of God, because we are out of His timing. We miss divine moments and opportunities, simply because we are not standing still at the Lord's command. We forfeit seasons and times of God because we are too busy; our eyes are not looking to God—the Author and Finisher, the Author and Perfector, the One who started this journey with us and knew the storms would be raging; however, He has promised to faithfully complete this journey with us.

The children of Israel came out of hard labour and the journey through the wilderness was long and exhausting. They were finally out of bondage only to find themselves in a seemingly impossible situation. They just needed to be quiet for a bit in order to reflect on what God had done, and gather strength and faith in order to believe that God would also see them through yet another challenge.

When God tells us to stand still, He just wants us to rest and be at peace; and recuperated in order that we might move forward in His strength. In that time of standing still, God expects us to ponder and reflect on what He has done in the past, reflect on His past deliverances and provision; and mediate on the miracles he performed when we were in *'Egypt'*. On meditation and reflection we become inspired and recharged, with our minds renewed to begin the journey again; when He tells us to move forward.

This also time of resting and standing still is a time of prayer, praise, worship, fasting and meditation on God's word, works and promises. In this space we shut the door and our ears to the noisy winds of Baal Zephon; and open our ears to the still voice of the Holy Spirit and our good Shepherd—Jesus Christ. God will do it again in your life. Wonders have not ceased! Miracles have not ceased! Signs have not ceased in the kingdom of God! God does not take a holiday, He keeps a twenty four hour watch over us; and is at work twenty four hours a day.

We might not see Him working with our physical eyes, however the song writer wrote;

Lord, I believe in You
I'll always believe in You
Though I can't see You with my eyes
Deep in my heart
Your Presence I find
Lord, I believe in You
Tommy Walker

God does no go into retirement; we can always find Him when we by faith look deep inside us; and look into His word of truth—The Holy Bible. Look to God and find Him and His works through faith and belief. Faith and belief are pre-requisites for Godly wisdom and understanding.

Know that He who has taken us thus far is more than able to keep us, sustain us and bring us to our destination in Him. I can just hear the song of David when he said, *"I will lift up mines eyes to the hill from whence comes my help? My help comes from the Lord, Who made heaven and earth"* (Psalm 12:1-2 NKJV). Gather strength, because the journey ahead is greater, and as a result the battles and storms are tougher. So, take time to stand still and watch God move whilst you recuperate from your previous challenges and battles.

CHAPTER 10

Stormy Winds, Fulfilling His Words

Maybe right now the "stormy winds" of adversity are creating chaos in your ministry, home, marriage, finances, health and employment. I have great news for you straight from the Word of God. Those "stormy winds" are helping to propel the fulfilment of God's promises in your life. You're being equipped for a higher level in God—more grace is being given you for today's race, while fresh oil is being released into your life.

The Psalmist wrote,

Praise the Lord from the earth, You great sea creatures and all the depths; Fire and hail, snow and clouds; Stormy wind, fulfilling His word; (Psalms 148:7-8 NKJV).

God is admonishing everything that has breath to praise Him. He created everything both visible and invisible, and can speak to all nature so that it must obey His commands. Take a praise break this very minute, offering up high praises to the King of kings and the Lord of lords, and watch the King of glory inhabit your praises and bring a divine turnaround in your life!

Daniel 3 details the story of Shadrach, Meshach and Abed-Nego—three Hebrew boys who were thrown into a fiery furnace, all because they refused to bow down to a graven image that was foreign to the will of God for their destinies. These boys didn't hesitate to maintain their allegiance to The ONE TRUE GOD, without giving thought to the cost. They didn't compromise their faith, though they were facing certain death. The loss of their lives wasn't even a passing thought as they held fast to the unfailing promises of God.

Enraged at their attitude, King Nebuchadnezzar commanded that they be thrown into a fiery furnace that was seven times hotter than the norm, according to the Word of God. The king and his subjects were suddenly astonished when they saw not only the three bound men who were cast in the fiery furnace, walking around loose in the fire, but they also witnessed a fourth man walking around beside them.

King Nebuchadnezzar and his subjects failed to comprehend that the God who created all things, visible and invisible, was more than able to command the elements and they had to obey Him. Furthermore, He is the God who answers by fire; and the God who Himself is a consuming fire *(1 Kings 18:24, 37-39, Hebrews 12:29).*

Regardless of what the enemy throws at us to deter us from our God-given assignments, Jesus will always step right in and turn it around for our good, so that His name will be praised, honoured and lifted high above all else. Rejoice, for the enemy's minions, sent to increase the heat of our current trials, will shift. Like the Hebrew men in the fire, the enemy will be devoured by the scorching flames they prepared for us.

God's Word encourages us with yet another promise:

When you pass through the waters, I will be with you; And through the rivers, they shall not overflow you. When you walk through the fire, you shall not be burned, Nor shall the flame scorch you. For I am the Lord your God, The Holy One of Israel, your Saviour; I gave Egypt for your ransom, Ethiopia and Seba in your place. (Isaiah 43:2-3 NKJV) Be encouraged today, no matter how your "stormy winds" present themselves, just laugh at the enemy and his cohorts, and offer sacrificial praises to God for fulfilling His promises on your behalf. You might find it difficult to smile, let alone laugh. However, that's exactly why it's called sacrificial. The joy of the Lord is our strength. Why? When you begin to rejoice and make melody to the Lord, you'll find that the presence of the Lord will bring you to a place of unspeakable peace and joy, that will strengthen you in the midst of the fire and the storm. Strength comes from rejoicing in the Lord.

Like the Hebrew men, you won't be destroyed by the fire or the storms. In fact, you'll come out of it, without even smelling like smoke. I'm sure you can recall the many times God has delivered you when no one else was even aware of the danger. Many who saw you were in awe of your testimony because they saw no signs of your struggle. Was there ever such a time that you can recall? In this trial, the same God who delivered you yesterday, will deliver you today and even in the future. When God delivers you, you will look neither battered nor bruised.

Jesus was made manifest to you and me,

To console those who mourn in Zion, To give them beauty for ashes, The oil of joy for mourning, The garment of praise for the spirit of heaviness; That they may be called trees of righteousness, The planting of the Lord, that He may be glorified" (Isaiah 61:3 NKJV). At the end of it all, men will witness and bear testimony of the peace and joy of the Lord in our lives. The smell of fire will be nowhere to be found in your dwellings; rather, our lives will radiate the beauty and glory of God. Praises will be continually on our lips, as we daily glorify God for the marvellous works He has done and will do in our lives, no matter what storms come our way.

ARE YOU SEEKING A HIDING PLACE FROM THE STORMS OF LIFE?

Where is your boat at this very moment? Is it being tossed to and fro on life's heavy seas, with nowhere to hide from the high waves that threaten to capsize it? The water in the sea might be dark as the enemy continues to throw massive obstacles into the sea around us.

Are you in great despair and at the point of giving up, accepting defeat? I encourage you that your divine protector, the God who is the Creator of the earth, is always present to hide you under the shadow of His almighty wings, keeping you safe until the storm passes by.

Stand on and claim the promises of God which will never fail. You might be going through seemingly endless heartache that has you feeling weak and exhausted, but God is there when you call on His name, and will grab hold of the situation, turning it around for your good.

God will never give you over to the will of the enemy or cause them to prevail over you. The Psalmist wrote,

Why do the nations rage, And the people plot a vain thing? The kings of the earth set themselves, And the rulers take counsel together, Against the Lord and against His Anointed, saying, «Let us break Their bonds in pieces And cast away Their cords from us.» He who sits in the heavens shall laugh; The Lord shall hold them in derision. Then He shall speak to them in His wrath, And distress them in His deep displeasure: *(Psalms 2:1-5 NKJV).*

The enemy will take counsel against you to destroy you, the Lord's anointed. The devil will stop at nothing to break into pieces and destroy all you have and all you are in God. Life's storms and seas will rage against us and threaten our lives and destinies. However, God sits and laughs at our enemies and His enemies, because He knows that the devil and his cohorts are no match to Him, His Power and His Word! *When the wicked spring up like grass, and when all the workers of iniquity flourish, it is that they may be destroyed forever. (Psalms 92:7)* Hence, the Lord laughs at the folly of the wicked; who set themselves up only to be destroyed by the Almighty God. Faithful is He who has promised; and your safety, deliverance and victory will come to pass. If God be for us, then who can be against us? *(Hebrews 10:23, Romans 8:31).*

Whether you believe it or not, you are merely passing through the storm. We will walk through the valley of the shadow of death, however, the Word of God hidden in our hearts and our vessels will comfort and carry us through. God's rod and staff –His Word, will lead and usher us to the "other side"—a place of victory and triumph. As you face trials, be encouraged that you're not without a Saviour. Your Saviour—Jesus Christ is with you, and He is taking the journey with you.

The writer of Hebrews said this,

Looking unto Jesus, the author and finisher of our faith, who for the joy that was set before Him endured the cross, despising the shame, and has sat down at the right hand of the throne of God. (Hebrews 12:2) Jesus is the Author and Finisher of our life and our life's journey. Whatever He starts with us, He will finish, as long as we keep our gaze fixed on Him and not on the turbulence under our feet.

Like Jesus, there's joy and a breakthrough set before us. There is a victor's crown waiting for us at the end of this seemingly endless trial. The key to obtaining the prize, is endurance. Jesus endured the cross—and came through victorious, as will we.

Jesus despised the shame. How can someone despise shame? By rejecting it as shame and seeing it as a "stepping stone" to the destination God has for us. You and I can despise the shame by turning the negatives into positives, and allowing God to lead and guide us to His place of divine rest and recovery. Jesus despised the shame and was promoted to the right hand of God the Father, presiding over all things in heaven, on the earth and beneath the earth, He rightfully acquired a name above every other name, becoming the King of kings and Lord of lords, and Lord over all.

It wasn't easy for Christ to endure His trial. On one occasion Jesus prayed to the Father saying,

"O My Father, if it is possible, let this cup pass from Me; nevertheless, not as I will, but as You will." (Matthew 26:39b). Jesus told His disciples that His soul was sorrowful even unto death. *(Matthew 26:38)* He felt deep sorrow as His time was drawing nigh to be betrayed, imprisoned, mocked, spat upon, ridiculed and ultimately, crucified.

Your soul might be sorrowful and you might be asking God as it were, to remove this cup of suffering from you, or rescue you from your trial. Nonetheless, like our Lord Jesus, as you surrender to the Father's will, you'll be ushered into His promised blessings and experience the fulfilment of every promise God has made to you. Jesus understands your pain and sorrow, and He also knows that the glory ahead of you is far greater than the storm you're now facing.

David—a man not unfamiliar with diverse battles, betrayal, loss and stormy winds, wrote this:

You are my hiding place; You shall preserve me from trouble; You shall surround me with songs of deliverance. Selah. (Psalms 32:7 NKJV)

In the midst of his battles, the Lord became his shield, his hiding place, and the One who protected his life and destiny through it all. David was surrounded with "songs of deliverance." He made melody unto God at all times, knowing His God was more than able to deliver him. In fact, God surrounded David with songs of deliverance and delivered him out of all his troubles. He was always faithful to rescue His servant from every trial. His songs of deliverance were his testimony to the faithfulness of God in every trial.

I believe that each time David found himself in a dangerous situation, the first thing he did was praise and thank the Lord for His deliverance, before it was made manifest. David sang songs in faith to God, knowing God had never disappointed him and never would. In this trial, let God become your refuge and hiding place. Don't hide in dark shadows or bury your head in the sand of shame, reproach and despair. Hide in God and surround yourself with His Word. The name of the Lord is a strong tower into which the righteous run and find safety. Sing songs of deliverance as a reminder to God of what He has brought you through, and His promises to you.

Worship your way out of every bondage and trial. Praise your way out of every pain. Let your praises propel you to win the battle against the enemy. Praise and worship your way into the rest of God, even in the midst of the storm. In every storm there is what is known as an "eye". This is a calm region at the centre of a storm.

It's said that the strong surface winds that converge toward the centre never reach the "eye" of the storm.

Likewise, in the centre of every storm we face, there is that place of calm and quietness. In the midst of your trial, there's a place of peace that the strong winds never touch. Find that inner place of God's peace. Jesus said,

"Peace I leave with you, My peace I give to you; not as the world gives do I give to you. Let not your heart be troubled, neither let it be afraid" *(John 14:27).* Jesus not only gives us peace, but He leaves His peace with us—a peace no one can ever take away. Hence, as we face the "stormy winds", Jesus admonishes us not to let our hearts be troubled, neither let our hearts be afraid.

God's peace is the "eye" in the midst of our storms. We're neither troubled nor afraid as His peace is guaranteed. God's peace is an assurance of His love and faithfulness toward those who believe on Him. Allow the peace of the Lord to enter your heart and mind. Take comfort in His unfailing love and promises, believing you can do all things through Christ who strengthens you—including going through the storms by His grace.

Whilst Paul and the men were caught in a dangerous and life-threatening situation, Paul said,

"Then, fearing lest we should run aground on the rocks, they dropped four anchors from the stern, and prayed for day to come" (Acts 27:29). Prayer is one of the major keys that will not only assist us during the storms and trials, but it's also a vehicle that gets us to God's desired destination. "Praying for the day to come", involves not only petitioning God, but also speaking forth the commanded Word of Christ into our trials.

Rebuking the wind requires speaking the Word of God by faith to the wind. We ought to pray without ceasing as commanded by the Lord. Pray until you see "daybreak" and pray after you enter "daybreak." Prayer not only rebukes the devil and causes the promise of God to be made manifest; prayer also preserves the blessings of God.

Once we enter our breakthrough, we ought not to stop praying. Not because our deliverance has come; we should just never stop praying. The devil never gives up on his quest to kill, steal and destroy us. Therefore, we can't afford to relax once the storm is over and "Euroclydon" has been destroyed. Remember that the devil is always planning another storm. Prayer protects our breakthroughs from the wiles of the enemy. Prayer strengthens us, preventing us from once again becoming victims of the devil's windstorms. The newness of God in us and the life of God in us are preserved and sustained by prayer after the storm is over.

We can't go quiet at all during the storm, nor can we relax and go quiet after the storm. Jesus once spoke a parable to His disciples saying,

"The kingdom of heaven is like a man who sowed good seed in his field; but while men slept, his enemy came and sowed tares among the wheat and went his way," The wheat and the tares sprouted and appeared together. When the servant asked his master how it was that he sowed good seed in his field, yet tares appeared; the master replied, "An enemy has done this" (See Matthew 13: 24-25, 24- 30).

As Jesus pointed out, good seeds were sown, but whilst men slept, the enemy sowed tares which contended with the good seed.

"While men slept" is likened to whilst men relax and refuse to pray; the enemy then sows evil things among the good God has done in our lives. We ought to be watchful and vigilant both during and after the storms. The devil goes around like a roaring lion seeking whom he may devour. The enemy goes to and fro considering who he might next afflict like Job. Believe it or not, God is more than able to sow good seeds during your times of trial. In fact, God does exactly that.

Never give the enemy an opportunity to sow that which will strangle the seed of God's Word in your life. Never allow prayerlessness to put out the light of God in you. During the storms of life, if you wish to cry and groan, cry and groan in the Spirit or heavenly language. In doing so the Holy Spirit makes intercession on your behalf. If we are going to speak, let's only declare the Word of God that is able to see us through and deliver us.

If all one can say is "Jesus! Jesus! Jesus!" Call upon His name by faith and watch the supernatural and miraculous take place in your life. The battle with the "stormy winds" and trials, is a battle of words. Use no woeful words, but the Word of God as written and spoken concerning your trials and the promises of God. Speak the Word of God against all the devil does and is doing in an effort to cause your boat to capsize.

The formula for your victory is a combination of prayer and praise as you go through the "stormy winds" and fire. Prayer and praise reinforce the Word of God and summon God's divine interventions. **PUSH** through the storms; **P**ray **U**ntil **S**omething **H**appens and **P**raise **U**ntil **S**omething **H**appens. Let your prayer push back the waves and high tides. Let diabolical flames and fires be put out as you declare the Word of God. God's Word says,

«*Is not My word like a fire?*» *says the Lord,* «*And like a hammer that breaks the rock in pieces? (Jeremiah 23:29).* God's Word consumes and devours every diabolical fire that is lit in our lives, and breaks into pieces every plan the devil orchestrates against us.

Paul and Silas who were once imprisoned, began praying, and singing hymns to God. Whilst doing so the Bible tells us,

But at midnight Paul and Silas were praying and singing hymns to God, and the prisoners were listening to them. Suddenly there was a great earthquake, so that the foundations of the prison were shaken; and immediately all the doors were opened and everyone's chains were loosed. (Acts 16: 25-26) Paul and Silas were praying and singing to God at midnight and in their dark season. The prison doors opened and chains were loosed. Men including Paul and Silas were loosed and set free all because they chose to pray, praise and worship in their midnight hour.

You might be imprisoned by the storm, but I encourage you to pray and praise—apply God's victory formula and expect God to move "suddenly" on your behalf and on behalf of others, including your family and loved ones. The prisoners were listening and watching the servants of God. In the same way, others are watching and listening to you as you battle through the stormy winds. The question is: what are you saying? What are those looking on going to see and hear coming from you?

Are those watching you and depending on you for their deliverance hearing songs and words of woe and lamentation? Are they hearing negative utterances coming from you and seeing you crumble in the midst of adversity? Or, can they hear you making a joyful noise unto the Lord and declaring His goodness and promises no matter what?

The song writer poured his heart out to the Lord in his dark moments and times of storms, when he wrote,

When peace like a river, attendeth my way
When sorrow like sea billows roll
Whatever my lot, thou hast taught me to say
It is well, it is well with my soul
Horatio Spafford

Horatio Spafford was a man who experienced great storms and boisterous winds, resulting in actual loss of life, yet he penned such a beautiful song that today, is a testimony to God's love, peace and faithfulness. What is your song and what is your praise? What is your declaration? Fire and hail, snow and clouds, stormy winds— no matter the weather conditions of life, God's Word WILL be fulfilled.

Printed and bound by CPI Group (UK) Ltd, Croydon, CR0 4YY